Collins

need to know?

Barry Grossman

Collins

First published in 2006 by HarperCollins Publishers
Westerhill Road
Bishopbriggs
Glasgow
G64 2QT

www.collins.co.uk

Collins® is a registered trademark of
HarperCollins Publishers Limited

10 09 08 07 06
 5 4 3 2 1

A catalogue record for this book is available from
the British Library

For the Publishers: Morven Dooner
                     Elaine Higgleton
                     Lorna Knight
Designer: Gordon MacGilp
Series design: Mark Thomson
Photographer: Wes Kingston

ISBN-13: 978-0-00-723509-4
ISBN-10: 0-00-723509-7

Colour reproduction by Colourscan, Singapore
Printed and bound by Printing Express Ltd,
Hong Kong

Contents

Introduction

Games are strange things. Some, like chess and backgammon, look terribly complicated to an onlooker who doesn't know the rules. It seems like you must have to be some sort of expert to play these games.

In fact, this isn't the case; it doesn't take long to learn how to push chess pieces or backgammon counters round the board in accordance with the laws of the game, although you will get a lot more out of it (and in the case of backgammon, which is fundamentally a gambling game, do your bank balance a lot less harm) if you achieve a reasonable degree of skill.

Scrabble is different somehow. Even if someone had never seen the game in their life before, it probably wouldn't take them long to pick up the general idea if they watched a game being played. The scoring might take them a little longer, but fundamentally, it's easy enough – just place the letters on the board to form words, like in a crossword. This makes most people think that once they've grasped that, they know all they need to know – perhaps all there is to know – about the game.

This is very far from the truth. Scrabble, like chess or backgammon, like bridge, golf, or cross-country skiing, has a high skill factor. And that doesn't just mean knowing lots of words. Thinking that the player with the biggest vocabulary will automatically win a Scrabble game is like saying the bigger bloke will

good to know

In a two-person game, most people playing with family and friends will average between 180 and 300 points per game. Stronger players can average more than 400 points.

good to know

The highest-ever score for a single word was 392 for CAZIQUES, played by Karl Khoshnaw of Richmond, Surrey in 1982. The highest score for a game is a massive 1049 by Phil Appleby of Lymington, Hampshire.

always win a boxing match. Other things being equal, that may be true. But who would you back if the World lightweight champion fought Johnny Vegas?

A strong player will certainly know a lot of words that the average person, even the average reasonably well-educated person, will never have heard of. But you have to know the right words. A professor of English will find it no help at all in Scrabble to know words like **CATACHRESTICAL** or **SOMNILOQUENCE**. You can beat the Prof if you know words like **OURIE** and **ZAX**.

A game of Scrabble is basically a series of problems. How many times have you yelled in frustration at picking too many vowels or consonants, or cursed the fates for giving you an unwanted J, Q, X, or Z? How often have you looked at the tiles on your rack and thought 'I bet these make a seven-letter word', but not been able to work out what it was? How much more fun would the game be if you knew how to deal with these situations?

Making the most of 'good' tiles on your racks and limiting the damage from 'bad' ones is what makes your game more enjoyable, and improve your chances of winning. And that's what this book is all about.

It won't happen automatically. It'll take a bit of concentration, a bit of practice, a bit of memory work. But if you enjoy Scrabble already, reading this book and taking on board what it suggests will bring you a lot more success at the game, and – more importantly – a lot more pleasure.

good to know

In 1985, two Royal Marines on a training exercise on Brabant Island, Antarctica, fell down a crevasse; luckily, one of them had a Scrabble set in his kitbag and they passed the five days that they waited to be rescued playing Scrabble.

good to know

There are daily or weekly puzzles or columns based on Scrabble in the Times, Daily Telegraph, Daily Mail and Daily Express. And, because its Orthodox readers cannot write on a Saturday, the Jewish Chronicle has a weekly crossword designed to be done by placing tiles on a Scrabble board.

1 From small beginnings...

Who invented Scrabble? Things used to be invented by the British. Now they are invented by the Japanese. But Scrabble turns out to be as American as apple pie.

History

Scrabble was first thought of in the 1930s. Alfred Butts was an architect, but unemployed owing to the Depression. He was also a word-game enthusiast. He did crosswords and enjoyed tinkering with anagrams. Hoping to make some money, he developed a game called Lexiko.

This involved players drawing seven tiles, then simply taking turns to discard tiles and draw new ones until they could make a seven-letter word. The first player to do so won. There was no board, no points, and no element of interlocking your word with what had already been played. No games manufacturer was interested in producing it, partly because in the Depression most people presumably had little money to spend on games, but partly, one suspects, because it sounds a bit boring.

Butts then introduced point values for the different letters. When a player had won a round by playing a seven-letter word, the others could play off whatever words they could make from their hand, and lose the point values of the remaining tiles, making it more or less a word version of rummy.

Determined as ever, Alfred tried again to have the game produced commercially, but still with no success.

As an architect, Butts would have known that everything takes time, whether building a house or perfecting a game. He kept refining his invention, and eventually added the board, the premium squares, and the crossword-style building up of words that we know from the game today.

By now, you might think that the manufacturers would have been falling over themselves to produce the game, but still Butts had no success. In 1939 he met James Brunot, a Government worker with an entrepreneurial streak. Brunot was immediately intrigued by the game. He played around with the idea, refined it a bit more, and, like Butts, tried to get

good to know

Scrabble has previously been known as Lexiko, Criss-Crosswords and It.

it onto the market. But it was now the early 1940s, and the world had more pressing matters to attend to. Finally, in 1949, Brunot formed his own business, the Production and Marketing Company, and the game – by now, after a few more name changes, called Scrabble – was finally ready to go into the shops.

Unfortunately, even after eighteen years or so of development, Scrabble was still no overnight success. Sales were slow, and Brunot was losing money. In the first three years, no more than 20,000 sets were sold. Things were looking grim for Alfred and James, and Scrabble might well have faded away there and then. Then Jack Strauss went on holiday.

Strauss was a shopkeeper, and he discovered Scrabble while on a summer break with some friends. He loved the game and, on his return to work, promptly placed an order and organized a major promotion for the game in the store. This might not have mattered much if Jack Strauss had just been any shopkeeper. In fact, he was the chairman of Macy's, one of the largest department stores in New York. With that kind of power to push it, Scrabble was well and truly on its way. Sales in the low thousands were transformed into millions, and Brunot's and Butts's long struggle was over.

Scrabble soon spread through the English-speaking world, and it wasn't long until the game was being produced in foreign languages too. Of course, this required a re-evaluation of the point values and frequency of each tile for every new language. If you struggle without an E, spare a thought for the Dutch, who are such E addicts that they have a whopping eighteen of them in a set, but

good to know

Butts based the frequency of letters in the Scrabble set on how often each occurred in headlines in *The New York Times*.

only twenty other vowels in total. A Russian set has thirty-three different letters represented, plus two blanks. Not surprisingly they couldn't shoehorn all those letters into ninety-eight tiles, and Russian Scrabble has a mighty 126 tiles per set, including the blanks. Their games must take quite a while to play, but then they have got those long Russian winters to get through.

Scrabble is now played by millions of people across the world, and it regularly tops the chart of best-selling games. About a hundred million sets have been sold worldwide since it all started in 1948. A hundred million! Walk into any house in Britain, and there's a one in two chance that it will have a Scrabble set lurking somewhere. The game is said to be popular in homes ranging from Buckingham Palace to prisons. Kylie Minogue is a big fan, and snooker players use it to relax in the long intervals between matches – Steve Davis and James Wattana are reported to be particularly hot, clearly masters of the Q as well as the cue.

Parents can introduce young children to the game with *My First Scrabble*, and then they can move on to *Junior Scrabble* when they are a little older. There is also a Braille version of the game, with raised dots on the tiles and the premium squares.

And nowadays, of course, no range is complete without the computer version. You can buy a CD-Rom to play against your computer, choosing an appropriate skill level so that you always (luck permitting) get a good, close game. But be warned, the computer version of the game is addictive. Many people have fallen into the 'just one more game' trap, only to look up several hours later to find the

good to know

Other foreign languages in which Scrabble is available include:
Afrikaans
Arabic
Danish
Finnish
Portuguese
Yiddish

dog unwalked, the shopping not done, or that multi-million pound business deal slipping past its deadline.

Alfred Butts died in 1993, so he lived long enough to see the worldwide success the game had become. Millions of sets, addicts by the tens of thousands, even Scrabble clubs and World Championships – could he have dreamt what he was starting when he came up with his curious little game, back in those dark, depressed days of 1931?

good to know

in 1998, to celebrate the game's 50th anniversary, two teams from the Army and the Navy played a game on the pitch at Wembley Stadium. The board was 30 m² and each tile was 1.5 m².

| 👥 | 10+ |
| 🧑‍🤝‍🧑 | 2-4 |

BBLE

...AY

...RD COUNTS! Play consists of
...r 2, 3 or 4 players. Play consists of
...crossword fashion, on the
...sing letter tiles with various score
...ame is to get the highest score. Each
...heir tiles in combinations and
...vantage of letter values and premium
...e combined total score for a game
...00 points to 800 or more, depending on

CONTENTS

...tiles with letters of the alphabet and two

...e letter tiles has score values indicated by the
...o the bottom right of the letter.
...blank tiles have no score value, and can be used as
...r desired. When it is played, the player must state
...etter it represents, after which it cannot be changed
...e remainder of the game.

SET UP

...t a pen and paper to keep score.
...et up the board in the middle of the playing area.
...ach player takes a rack for arranging their tiles and places
...t in front of them.

...All the tiles are placed in the tile bag. Each player takes a
...tile out to find out who plays first. The player who has the
...tile nearest the beginning of the alphabet, with the blank
...preceding 'A,' plays first. The exposed tiles are put back
...into the bag and the bag is shaken to shuffle them.

• Each player, in turn, then draws seven new tiles and places
  them on their racks. Everyone is now ready to play
  SCRABBLE®. Play proceeds clockwise.

RULES OF PLAY

Keeping score
One player is elected as scorekeeper. They keep tally of each
... player's score after each turn.

Exchanging tiles
Any player may use their turn to replace any or all of the tiles in
their rack. They may do so by discarding them face down,
drawing the same number of new tiles, then mixing the
discarded tiles with those remaining in the bag. They then await
their next turn to play.

Passing (missing a turn)
Instead of placing tiles on the board, or exchanging tiles, a player
may also decide to pass, whether or not they are able to make a
word (or words).

...However, should all players pass twice in succession, the game
... ...ore of their tiles to form a
... ...d either across or
... ...onal words

2 The rules of the game

Every set contains a copy of the rules, but just in case you've lost yours, or you haven't actually got yourself a Scrabble set yet (for shame!), this chapter gives you a quick guide.

Rules

1. Open out the board and give each player one of the tile racks. The bag containing the tiles should be placed to one side of the board, within easy reach of all the players.

need to know

LETTER	NUMBER IN SET	POINTS VALUE
A	9	1
E	12	1
I	9	1
O	8	1
U	4	1
B	2	3
C	2	3
D	4	2
F	2	4
G	3	2
H	2	4
J	1	8
K	1	5

2. One player acts as score-keeper, and will need a pen and paper. (Alternatively, all players can keep score as a check.)

3. Each player draws one tile from the bag. The nearest to the beginning of the alphabet starts. In the event of a tie, the tied players draw again. A blank beats an A. The letters are then put back in the bag and the bag is shaken.

4. The player who starts picks seven tiles from the bag, and places them on his or her rack without letting the other players see them. Passing to the left, the other players in turn also pick seven tiles and place them on their rack.

The first move

5. The first player combines from two to seven of his or her letters to form a word, and places that word on the board, either across (from left to right) or down (from top to bottom). One letter must go on the centre square (in most sets this is marked with a star or similar marker). The player counts his or her score (see

scoring, below) and announces it, then draws as many tiles from the bag as he or she has just played, thus keeping seven tiles on the rack.

Second and subsequent moves

6. Play passes to the left. Each player makes his or her move by adding from one to seven of their own tiles to those already on the board. The letters played, either across or down, must themselves form a valid word, and they must interlock with the letters already on the board, crossword-style, so that all additional words formed are also valid words. Again, the move is completed by the counting and announcing of the score, and the replenishment of the rack back to seven tiles by picking from the bag.

Scoring

7. The basic score for each tile is shown by a small number, from one to ten, printed in the bottom right-hand corner of the tile.

8. A letter placed on a **Double Letter Score** square has its value doubled; a letter placed on a **Triple Letter Score** square has its value tripled; if any letter of a word has been placed on a **Double Word Score** square that whole word has its entire score doubled, and if any letter

need to know *continued*

LETTER	NUMBER IN SET	POINTS VALUE
L	4	1
M	2	3
N	6	1
P	2	3
Q	1	10
R	6	1
S	4	1
T	6	1
V	2	4
W	2	4
X	1	8
Y	2	4
Z	1	10
Blank	2	0

good to know

Some 'house rules' allow players to consult a Dictionary *before* playing their move. This should be allowed very sparingly, if at all – perhaps for non-native speakers using the game to improve their English, and even then for a limited time only.

good to know

Another rule some people like to incorporate is to allow the blank to be lifted from the board and replaced with the letter it represents, allowing the player to re-use the blank. While not part of the official rules, this is a useful way to keep the game moving, and I would not discourage it, particularly for beginners.

of a word has been placed on a **Triple Word Score** then the word has its entire score tripled.

9. When two or more words are formed in one move, each is scored. The common letter is counted (with full premium values, if any) in the score for each word.

10. Premium squares are only counted in the move in which they are covered. If the word is modified in a subsequent move, tiles on premium squares count at face value only.

11. Any player playing all seven of his or her tiles in one move scores a bonus of fifty points in addition to the regular score for the move.

Miscellaneous

12. There are two blank tiles in the set, which may be used as any letter. When a blank is played, the player must nominate which letter the blank represents. The blank then remains as that letter for the rest of the game. A blank tile has a score of zero, but if a blank is placed on a Double Word or Triple Word square, the word is still doubled or tripled, as appropriate.

13. Rather than playing any tiles on the board, a player may instead choose to

change any or all of his or her tiles. To do this, the player places the tiles to be changed to one side, picks the same number of new tiles from the bag, then puts the old tiles back in the bag. A change counts as a score of zero, and a player cannot change and make a scoring move in the same turn.

14. Any other player may challenge a player's move, if he or she considers that any of the words made are not valid words. A challenge must be made before the player has picked and looked at any of the replacement tiles. The word should then be checked in a dictionary or an official Scrabble word source. If the word is wrong, the player must take back his or her tiles from that move, and gets a score of zero.

Ending the game

15. When there are no tiles left in the bag, play continues until one player has used all the tiles on his or her rack. Every other player then has the total value of their unplayed tiles deducted from their score, and the player who has played all his or her tiles has the total value of all unplayed tiles added to his or her score. If no player can play off all their tiles, each player has the value of their unplayed tiles deducted from their score.

good to know
It's difficult to assess how many words the average English speaker knows or uses, but estimates range from 40,000 to 75,000. Yet there are a whopping 267,633 words eligible for Scrabble in English! Lots to learn then...

Some example moves

Move 1 GATE scores 5, doubled, scores **10 points**.

Move 2 PITCH, with the **I** and **C** doubled, scores **16 points**.

Move 3 **GLARED**, with the **G** and **E** tripled, score 14, plus 6 for **AGATE**, scores **20 points.**

Move 4 **GRAPH**, with the **H** tripled, scores **19 points.**

Move 5 BIOGRAPHER scores **18 points.** (Note the H is not retripled.)

Move 6 OMIT scores 6 and **ID** scores 3, both doubled, making 18. **ME** scores 4 and **OR** 2, for a total score of **24 points**.

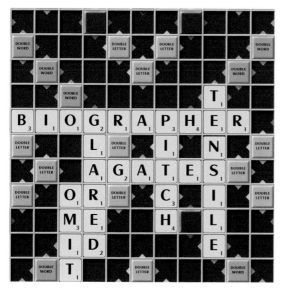

Move 7 TENSILE, covering two double word squares, is doubled then redoubled, scoring 7 x 4 = 28, plus 7 for **AGATES**, scores **35 points.**

Move 8 The **T** of **HONESTY** is doubled, then the whole word is doubled, scoring 20 (with the **H** as a blank scoring zero). Add 19 for **BIOGRAPHERS**, plus the 50-point bonus for using all seven tiles, for a total score of **89 points.**

You may not spot words like **BIOGRAPHER**, **HONESTY**, and **TENSILE** right away, but these moves have been shown to demonstrate the variety of ways you can 'build' a move within the basic rules, and how to score them.

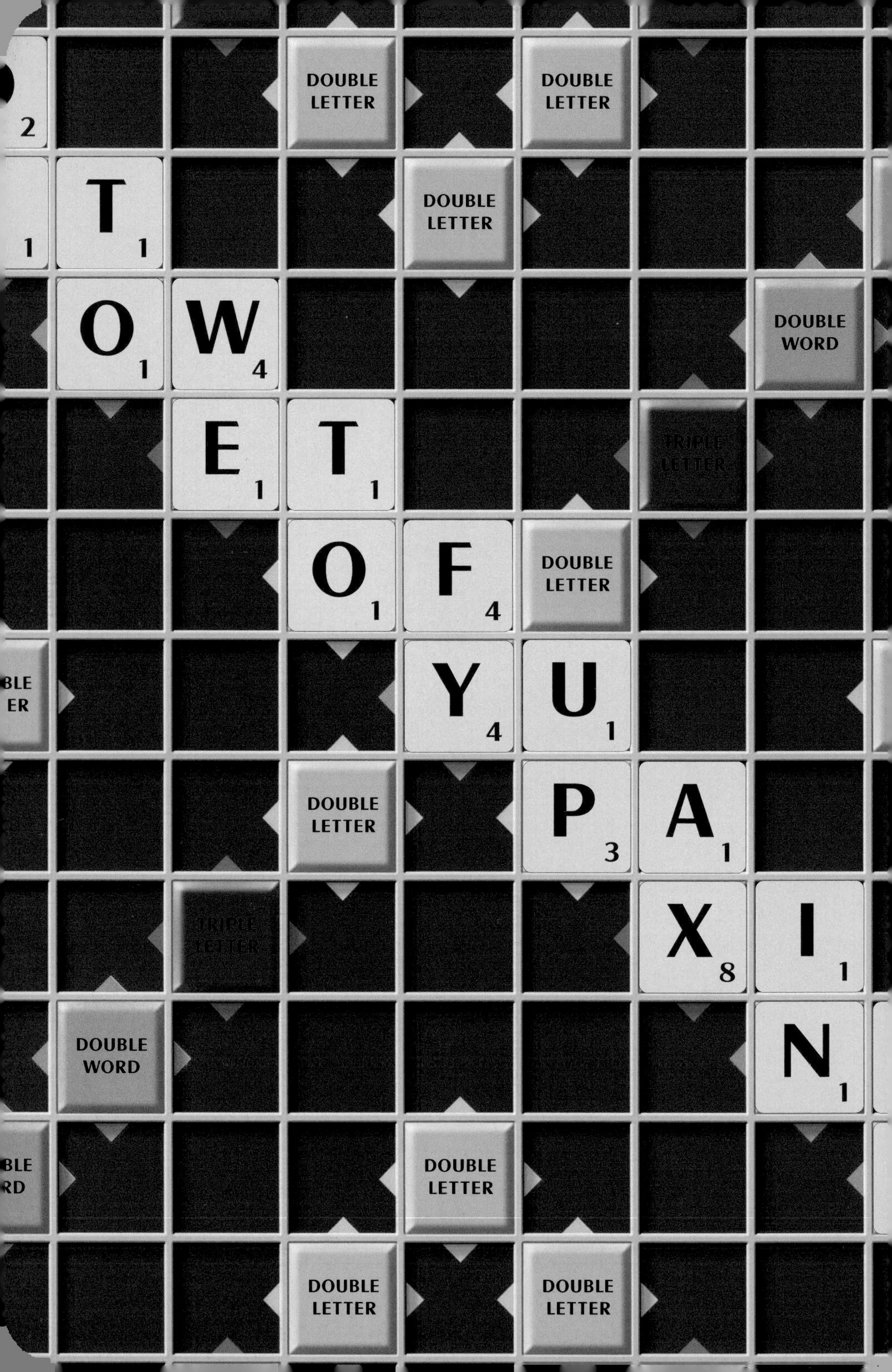

2

1

T 1

1

O 1   W 4

E 1   T 1

O 1   F 4

DOUBLE LETTER

DOUBLE LETTER

DOUBLE LETTER

DOUBLE WORD

TRIPLE LETTER

Y 4   U 1

BLE ER

DOUBLE LETTER

P 3   A 1

TRIPLE LETTER

X 8   I 1

DOUBLE WORD

N 1

BLE RD

DOUBLE LETTER

DOUBLE LETTER

DOUBLE LETTER

3 Two- and three-letter words

Now that we've got the rules sorted out, it's time to take a look at how you can improve your game. A major part of that consists of having a large armoury of useful words at your disposal. And the big word there is 'useful'.

2s and 3s

Where many people go wrong is that they think the longer a word is, the better it is to know, as it's likely to score more. In fact, the key to a good Scrabble vocabulary is a good knowledge of short words.

The reason for that is you can use the short words to 'hook' the word you want to play on to the board, allowing you to play parallel to another word, rather than always going through it crosswise. That way you will usually make more than one word each shot, gaining you a higher score.

BAD PLAY

Notice how by using the same letters from your rack, you have scored seventeen more points. But notice also that little word **FA** which enabled you to fit the play in. And there we have the first, essential thing you have to know to improve your game: **all the allowable two-letter words.** Yes, all of them.

There are 124 of them in *Collins Official Scrabble Dictionary*, but to make the list more manageable, you can divide them into three groups:

1. The ones you already know.

2. The ones you already know, but may not have realized were words.

3. The ones you probably don't know.

3 Two- and three-letter words

There are thirty-seven two-letter words which most people would know and which would appear in most dictionaries:

AH	AM	AN	AS	AT	AX	AY	BE	BY	DO	EH	GO
HA	HE	HI	HO	IF	IN	IS	IT	LA	LO	MA	ME
MY	NO	OF	OH	ON	OR	OX	PA	SO	TO	UP	US
WE											

So straight away you only have eighty-seven new ones to learn. But it's not even as bad as that, because now we move on to the second group: the ones you know, but don't know you know. These include:

Contractions:

AD (advertisement)   **PO** (chamberpot)

BI (bisexual)   **RE** (regarding)

MO (moment)   **TA** (thank you)

OP (operation)

AW	ER	HM	MM	OI	OW	OY
SH	ST	UH	UM	UR	YA	YO

Interjections and exclamations.

AR	EF	EL	EM	EN	ES	EX

Letters.

Then add in **ID** (the psychiatric term), **PI** (the Greek letter and mathematical term), and **YE** (the old form of **YOU**), and that's another thirty-one taken care of with no trouble at all.

Fifty-six to go. These are the ones you probably don't know, so let's set them out where you can get the measure of them:

AA	AB	AE	AG	AI	AL	BA	BO	CH	DA	DE	DI
EA	ED	EE	ET	FA	FE	FY	GI	GU	IO	JA	JO
KA	KI	KO	KY	LI	MI	MU	NA	NE	NU	NY	OB
OD	OE	OM	OO	OS	OU	PE	QI	SI	TE	TI	UG
UN	UT	WO	XI	XU	YU	ZA	ZO				

If all this looks a bit gobbledygookish, you may be surprised to know that even some of these are more familiar to you than you might realize. An **AB** is an abdominal muscle, as in toning up your abs and your pecs. **MU**, **NU**, and **XI** are Greek letters (and **PE** and **TE** are letters from our alphabet). **OM** is what Buddhists chant as part of their prayers.

Having said that, it can't be denied that some of the definitions are real doozies. To go from start to finish, **AA** is a word from Hawaiian, meaning a rough volcanic rock. Its opposite, smooth volcanic rock, is called **PAHOEHOE**. And a **ZO** is a Himalayan cross-breed of a yak and a cow, also spelt **ZHO**, **DZO**, **DZHO**, or **DSO**, useful Scrabble words every man-jack of them. Now, where else but in Scrabble can you go from Hawaii to the Himalayas in one step?

Have a look back at the two-letter words every so often as you're going through the book. Once you're happy with the first two groups (i.e. the common ones, the contractions, the interjections, the letters, plus **ID**, **PI**, and **YE**), have a real go at mastering the unusual ones. They really are the essential first step to improving your game.

good to know

AE one

AG agriculture

AI shaggy-coated slow-moving South American animal

AL Asian shrub or tree

BA Ancient Egyptian symbol for the soul

BO exclamation used to startle or surprise someone

CH archaic form of eke (to lengthen or stretch)

DA Burmese knife

DE of, from

DI plural of deus (god)

EA river

ED editor

EE (Scots) eye

ET (dialect) ate

FA (music) fourth degree of any major scale

FE fee

good to know *continued*

FY exclamation of disapproval

GI loose-fitting white suit worn in judo and karate

GU type of violin used in Shetland

IO type of moth

JA (in South Africa) yes

JO (Scots) sweetheart

KA spirit dwelling as a vital force in man or a statue

KI Japanese martial art

KO (in New Zealand) traditional digging tool

KY (Scots) cows

LI Chinese measurement of distance

MI (music) third degree of any major scale

NA (Scots) no

NE nor

NY near

OB expression of opposition

OD hypothetical force formerly thought to be responsible for many natural phenomena

OE grandchild

OO (Scots) wool

OS mouthlike opening

OU man, chap

QI (in Oriental medicine) vital life force

SI (music) seventh degree of any major scale

TI (music) seventh degree of any major scale

UG to hate

UN one

UT the note C

WO woe

XU Vietnamese currency unit

YU jade

ZA pizza

But it doesn't end there. **Three-letter words** are almost as important as the twos for helping you build up your moves – and there are a lot more of them. Unless you have a lot of time and aptitude to study lists, or have a photographic memory, it will take you a few months to fully get to grips with the threes. Take them gradually, starting with the ones containing **J**, **Q**, **X**, and **Z**. You won't need to know all of them before your game starts improving.

Here are some of the most useful threes:

CONTAINING J

GJU	type of violin used in Shetland
JAP	to splash
JEE	mild exclamation of surprise
JIZ	wig
JOE	(Scots) sweetheart
RAJ	(in India) government
TAJ	tall conical cap worn as a mark of distinction by Muslims

CONTAINING Q

QAT	evergreen shrubs
QIS	plural of QI (vital life force)
QUA	in the capacity of
SUQ	open-air market place, e.g. in north Africa

CONTAINING X

DEX	dextroamphetamine
GOX	gaseous oxygen
HOX	to hamstring
KEX	any of several large hollow-stemmed umbelliferous plants, such as chervil
RAX	to stretch or extend
REX	king
VOX	voice
WEX	wax
WOX	wax
XIS	plural of xi (fourteenth letter in the Greek alphabet)
ZAX	axe

CONTAINING Z

You can remember some of the Z-threes in sets of two and three:

BEZ   part of a deer's horn

BIZ   business

CAZ   casual

COZ, CUZ   cousin

FEZ   tasselled cap

FIZ   fizz

MIZ   misery

MOZ   hex

SAZ   Middle Eastern stringed instrument

SEZ   informal spelling of 'says'

ZAG, ZIG   to change direction sharply

Other useful Z-threes:

ADZ   tool with an arched blade

DZO   animal that is a cross between a cow and a yak

JIZ   wig

ZAX   axe

ZEP   type of long sandwich

ZOA   independent animal bodies

ZOS   plural of zo (animal that is a cross between a cow and a yak)

good to know

AIA female servant in the East

AUA yellow-eye mullet

AUE Maori exclamation

AYU small Japanese fish

EAU river

UVA grape

VAU, VAV sixth letter of the Hebrew alphabet

These lists are not exhaustive, but they'll certainly be enough to get you started. You won't always be able to fit in a **QUIVER**, a **ZEBRA**, or an **ANNEX**, so you need to know a good selection of these shorter words to help you play your high-scoring letters– preferably for a more than face-value score.

Other useful threes are the ones which can help you get rid of awkward letters like **U** and **V**, or which allow you to shed excess vowels. You should try to remember:

AIA	**AUA**	**AUE**	**AYU**
EAU	**UVA**	**VAU**	**VAV**

Threes which are hooks of frequently-used twos are also helpful. By 'hooks', we mean words which can be formed by adding one letter at the beginning or end of another word. You'll find that you play **ZO** fairly often now that you know it, which is why it's especially good to know **AZO**, **DZO**, and **ZOA** – not necessarily to play them at one fell swoop, but to add the extra letter to an already-played **ZO**, making another word at right angles while you're doing it. If you look back at the example moves shown in the previous chapter, notice that we didn't just add an **A** to **GATE** to make **AGATE** – we made a whole new word, **GLARED**, as well. This is why these hook-words – of any length – are so useful. The lists of useful **JQXZ** words above have partly been compiled with hooks in mind. Here are a few more commonly-played twos, and the threes you can make from them:

AA: **AAH AAL AAS BAA**
    CAA FAA MAA

CH: **ACH CHA CHE CHI**
    ECH ICH OCH

HM: **HMM OHM**

KY: **KYE KYU SKY**

good to know

AAH to exclaim in surprise
AAL Asian shrub or tree
CAA (Scots) to call
FAA (Scots) fall
CHE dialect form of 'I'
CHI 22nd letter of the Greek alphabet
ECH, ICH
        to eke out
KYE Korean fundraising meeting
KYU (in judo) on of the five grades for inexperienced competitors
OHM unit of electrical resistance

By now, you're wondering what on earth these odd-looking words mean. As with the twos, some are more familiar than you might realize – **BAA** and **MAA** are the cries of a sheep and a goat, **CHA** is tea, **ACH** and **OCH** are what you say if you're annoyed in Scotland, **HMM** is what you say if you're puzzled, and **AAS** are two lots of rough volcanic rock.

But a word of advice here – don't get too hung-up on meanings. It's a familiar, plaintive cry when someone new to a Scrabble club has an unfamiliar word

need to know

The only letter which does not feature in any two-letter word is **V**. There are no twos ending in **C, J, K, Q,** or **Z.**

need to know

You can get rid of excess Is and Us with **IWI** (Māori tribe), **ULU** (type of knife), and **UTU** (a reward). Then use hooks to turn them into **KIWI, ZULU,** and **TUTU.**

played against them: 'What on earth does **that** mean?'. It only adds to their bafflement when, as often as not, the answer comes back, 'I don't know'. It comes back to what we said before – it's not knowing lots of words that wins you games, it's knowing the right words. Experienced players build up a stockpile of words that they know will prove useful to them again and again. Sometimes the words have interesting meanings which can help you remember them. But often it's just another fish or plant, or something that Spenser used in about 1583, and which has lain, dusty and unloved, in the back of the cupboard of English words ever since. Until, that is, Scrabble players came along, blew the dust off, and started using it. We will point out some of the meanings worth knowing as we go along, but there is no rule that says you have to know the meaning of every word you play and, at the risk of incurring the wrath of the purists, I would suggest that it's very often all right just to know the word because it's good for Scrabble and not to worry about the meaning.

Another reason it is not *de rigueur* to ask about meanings during a game is that you might seem to be fishing for useful information, such as whether the word is a noun, verb, or adjective, and therefore whether you can put an S or some other letter after it. The time to ask about meanings is after a game, not during it.

In the final chapter of this book, we'll be mentioning some of the things you can do if you want to get a bit more serious about your Scrabble. Not 'serious' in the sense of solemn and humourless – Scrabble should never be that – but in the sense of really improving your game and perhaps joining a Scrabble club. In that section we'll also tell you where you can find lists of all the three-letter words, and many more lists besides. But in the meantime, you're doing fine if you learn the twos and make a start on the threes highlighted in this chapter. You'll soon wonder how you ever managed to play without your **AIA**, your **AUA**, your **WEX**, and your **WOX**.

HAVE A GO

CHALLENGE NO. 1

Your rack: **A E G N O R S**

First, work out the seven-letter word you have on your rack. It shouldn't be too difficult – think of colours or fruit. But can you find two places to play it on the board shown? Remember those two-and three-letter words.

4 Dealing with the JQXZ

Many players don't like to pick 'the big tiles' –
J, Q, X, and Z. They think that because there are
fewer words in which to play them, they'll be
hard to get rid of, and perhaps even end up on
their rack at the end of the game, costing them
a handful of points. This is wrong. The big tiles
are, *usually*, good tiles to pick.

The Big Tiles

You have already seen the two-letter words and some of the threes containing J, Q, X, and Z. So right away you have an armoury of words that will help you play these tiles.

Get points with short words:

The good thing about these small words is that they may well help you play a big tile for a worthwhile score. At this point, it's worth repeating the twos containing 'the big four':

JA   JO   QI   AX   EX   XI   OX   XU   ZA   ZO

Have a look at this section of a board in play:

Your rack: **D E I K L Q U**

You could play **QUITE** using the **T** on the board, scoring sixteen. But with your new-found knowledge of **QI**, you can play **QI** both ways, slotting in another two-letter word as well for a very healthy sixty-five points.

Your rack: **D E I K L Q U**

In a similar way, how would you score more than sixty points with this board and rack?

Your rack: **A D F I J O P**

4 Dealing with JQXZ

Your rack: **A D F I J O P**

You should see right away that the Triple Letter square is the one which is going to pay the dividend. Playing the **J** alone to make **JO** scores twenty-five. But we want to play a word downwards as well to get the **J** tripled again. **JO** doesn't fit in this case because you can't have **OTE**, but there's no problem with **ATE**. So play **JA** downwards, also making **JO** and **ATE**, and you're getting somewhere – fifty-three points for doing very little. Even better, add the **P** to the end of **JA** making **JAP**, turning **LATE** into **PLATE**, and you've bagged yourself another ten – sixty-three for the move.

Always be on the look-out for these small but profitable moves when you have one of the big tiles. The **X**, which forms two-letter words with all the other vowels (**AX EX XI OX XU**), is particularly useful for this tactic.

Get points with longer words:

Another great way to get big scores with the big tiles is to look for 'double-letter-double-word' slots, or, even better, 'triple-letter-double-word' or 'double-letter-triple-word'. It works like this. Remember that if one of the letters in your word covers a Premium *Letter* square, and another covers a Premium *Word* square, the appropriate letter is doubled or tripled before the whole word. So it's another way of making a letter count for a mighty *six times* its face value. Your job is to make sure that it's a high-scoring tile that gets the six-times treatment. Have a look at this situation:

On you rack you are holding **EEINOS** plus one of the big tiles. Can you see where you could get your big tile doubled then redoubled, or doubled then tripled, or tripled then doubled, if it was a **J**, a **Q**, or a **Z**?

Of course, you need to be thinking here of rather longer words than the two- and three-letter ones we have been using up to now. But there are plenty of common five- and six-letter words, even with the big tiles in them, and none of the words you are looking for here is unusual.

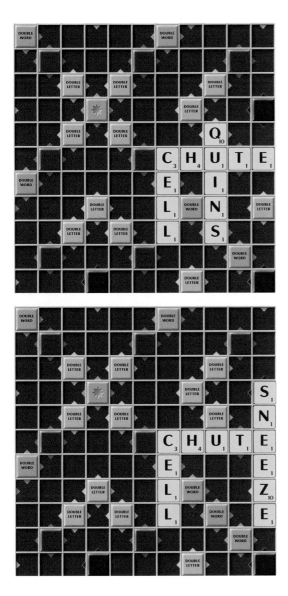

Score with JQXZ on the Triple Word:

If no opportunities like the ones shown above present themselves when you have a big tile, you can often get a good score simply by mopping up a handy Triple Word Square.

good to know

A few useful four- and five-letter words with **JQXZ**:

JUGA small processes at the base of forewings in certain insects

JORAM large drinking bowl

AFLAJ Plural of **FALAJ**

FALAJ water channel

AQUA water

QUATE fortune

QUINE a boisterous or disreputable woman

TRANQ tranquilizer

IXIA southern African plant of the iris family

PREX US college president

SOREX a shrew or related animal

XENIA influence of pollen upon the form of the fruit developing after pollination

ZEIN protein occurring in maize

ZILA administrative district in India

ZAIRE currency used in the former Zaire

Look at this position:

Ordinarily there wouldn't be much worth in taking this Triple Word square. With low-scoring tiles the score wouldn't amount to much, and, if the left-hand row is usable all the way to the top or bottom, you could be opening a good place for your opponent to score a high-scoring bonus. But if you can slot in **JET**, **QAT**, or **ZIT**, you pocket a handy thirty or thirty-six points, and you would be very unlucky if your opponent was ready to move in with an eight-letter word beginning or ending with the high-scoring tile you have provided. If your opponent does use the high-scorer to make a word that isn't a fifty-point bonus, it would be most unlikely to score as many as yours just has. It would quite likely be no more than twelve or fourteen points – a big net profit for you.

But the big tiles aren't always good:,

There are times when you don't want to pull one of these high-scorers out of the bag: when you're close to a bonus, and, sometimes, when you're close to the end of a game.

If you have six low-scoring tiles, well balanced between vowels and consonants, and with not too many duplicates, you should be well on your way to making a seven-letter bonus word. Picking **J**, **Q**, **X**, or **Z** at that stage just screws the whole thing up, unless you're lucky enough to pick, say, a **Z** to a rack of **AEINST**, which you can then arrange into **ZANIEST**. Usually you just have to play the high-scorer for a low score, if you follow me, such as plonking down the **Z** to make **ZO** for eleven points.

Sometimes you are faced with the dilemma of whether to break up your promising combination (**AEINST**, or whatever) for the sake of getting twenty-odd points for your high scorer rather than eleven or so. How much easier if you had drawn a nice **R** for **RETAINS** or **G** for **SEATING**. But in Scrabble, as in life, things don't always work out that way.

The other time you may not want to see a big tile heaving itself onto your rack is towards the end of the game. It depends on whether there is

need to know

You don't need a **U** to get rid of a **Q**: All the following words, mostly from Arabic, are allowed:

QI (in Oriental medicine) vital life force

QAT white-flowered evergreen shrub whose leaves have narcotic properties

QADI judge in a Muslim country

QAID chief

QOPH nineteenth letter of the Hebrew alphabet

WAQF endowment in Muslim law

FAQIR Muslim who spurns worldly possessions

QANAT underground irrigation channel

QIBLA direction of Mecca, to which Muslims turn in prayer

TALAQ Muslim form of divorce

somewhere to play it for at least twenty points or so. If there is, it can win you a close game. If not, you either have to play it off for what you can (possibly giving your opponent a chance to play out and leave you with the rest of your letters on your rack), or conversely, get rid of the rest of your letters for whatever you can and perhaps get stuck with the biggie. In some cases, if the board is blocked, you might not be able to get rid of it at all.

So you can think of picking the **JQXZ** tiles as being a bit like the phone ringing. Usually it's nice, like a friend ringing for a chat, or your girl- or boy-friend wanting to whisper sweet nothings in your ear. But occasionally it's nasty, like a friend ringing to ask if they can stay with you for a week, or your girl – or boy-friend wanting to whisper sweet nothings while your spouse is listening on the extension.

HAVE A GO

CHALLENGE NO. 2

Can you find a move that scores 45?
And can you find a move that scores over 55?

Your rack: **D E I J N O S**

CHALLENGE NO. 3

Your rack: **A E L M Q S U**

Can you score over 50 by playing six tiles?

In another part of the board, can you score over 60 by playing six tiles?

Can you achieve a higher score by playing fewer tiles?

5 Using the S and the blank

Although S is only worth one point, it's much more valuable than you might think, because it can help you form 7-letter words and score 50 bonus points. The blank square is also valuable for getting bonus scores.

Using the S

If you look at a game played between two good club players, and one between two less experienced players, a few differences will quickly be obvious.

1. The stronger players (the sort of player you are now on the way to becoming) will have played plenty of those unusual two- and three-letter words we have already looked at.

2. There will be more parallel plays, resulting in solid blocks of tiles, rather than words which criss-cross through each other.

3. There will be more seven- and eight-letter words played for fifty-point bonuses.

This chapter will focus on the third of these, and in particular, how to use the six best tiles in the set – the four **S**'s and the two blanks – to get them.

Why are the **S** and blank so useful? Let's start with the **S**. Look around you and come up with the first few words that come into your head. You might think of **chair, table, book, sit,** and **read**. Depending on who's in the room with you, you could come up with **man, woman, husband, wife, boy, girl**, or perhaps if you're in one of those categories of avid Scrabble players that we mentioned earlier, **prince** or **cellmate**.

And what does every one of those words have in common? Yes, you can put an **S** at the end of all of them. Even **man** (he mans the lifeboat), **woman** (to act like a woman or to staff with women), and **wife** (to become a wife or take a wife) are verbs which can have **S** after them (or 'take an **S**', as Scrabble players tend to say). As can nearly every noun and verb in the English language. Many of the smaller words take **S** even if it is not because of their status as a noun or verb – **DI** is a noun but is plural already (plural of **deus**, a god), but you can have **DIS**, teenage slang meaning to disrespect. Even a lot of words that end in **S** take an **S** – **PRINCES, POSSES, BRAS, NEEDLES**, and indeed **DIS. ZEBRAS** can become **ZEBRASS** (a cross between a zebra and an ass), and if you're ever in a game where **DEADLINE** is played, then someone makes it **DEADLINES**, you could well and truly flabbergast your opponent by turning that into **DEADLINESS**.

The relevance of all this to the **S** on your Scrabble rack is twofold. One, if you can make a six-letter word with the other six letters, chances are you'll be able to stick an **S** on the end of it and, hey presto, you've got a seven. So you've only got six letters to worry about manipulating. That means, assuming no blanks or duplicates, you only have 720 different ways to arrange your tiles which, while it might sound quite a lot, is a lot easier than the 5,040 ways you can arrange seven different tiles.

Of course, you may have a seven-letter word with an **S** in it, but the **S** isn't at the end; with a rack of **ILNORST** it may only be after coming up with wrong 'uns like litrons, nitrols, and trilons that you finally sniff out **NOSTRIL**. But the point is that it's worth putting your **S** at the end of the rack and thinking around the other six to start with, and only if that fails should you have to start getting more imaginative.

Second, once you've found your bonus word, you have a high chance of being able to fit it in. What

good to know

Don't forget that there are four S tiles in a set, so there's a reasonably high chance that you'll get one at some point in the game.

can match the desolation of working out a splendid seven and then not being able to get it down? But with all those other words already on the board, most of them taking an **S**, you will usually have a couple of positions onto which you can hook your brilliant bonus.

It is worth stressing here that you should not necessarily hang onto an **S** until you can get a bonus with it. Its usefulness for hooking means you can often get a good score with it without a bonus. Watch especially for positions where you can get two words doubled with the addition of an **S**.

If you have an **S** in this position, you should be looking to make whatever word you can with it, and use it to turn **FIRM** into **FIRMS**. If you can get a high-scorer on the Double Letter, so much the better. Something like **WRITS**, coming down to also make **FIRMS**, would score forty-four.

So, to summarise, the S can:

1. Allow you to play a word, hooking an existing word, and thus scoring for both.
2. Increase your chance of finding a seven-letter word.
3. Taking 1 and 2 together, it can increase your chance of finding a playable 7-letter word.

The two S's problem

So, if one **S** is good, it follows that two on your rack at the same time must be twice as good. Right? Wrong!

Why? Well, quite simply, two of anything on your rack tends to weaken it (leaving aside blanks, which we'll come to in a moment). It's all to do with those different combinations again – you have far fewer separate ways of arranging your letters if you have a duplicate.

good to know

SDEIGN old form of disdain

SGRAFFITI ceramic objects that are decorated with patterns incised in to the top layer of the glaze to reveal parts of the ground

SHADDOCK edible yellow fruit that's a bit like a grapefruit

SHOOKS plural of SHOOK (set of parts ready for assembly)

SPINK finch

SPROD young salmon

Two **E**'s are usually all right, because the **E** is such a common letter in English. And two **S**'s are certainly better than some other duplicates; the dreaded duplicate **V** or **U** are real killers. But a second **S** has basically lost its advantage of being an **S** – its essential 'essness' (no, not a valid word). If you put one **S** to one side, hoping to make a word with the other six letters, and then stick the **S** at the end of it to make a seven, what has happened is that your second **S** has turned into just another letter. You're not really very likely to pick in **ZEBRASS**, and if you get all four **S**'s for **POSSESS** you might find your opponent complaining to the Monopolies Commission.

As it happens, the most common *initial* letter for a word in *Collins Scrabble Dictionary* is, you've guessed it, **S**, and by quite a long way. So yes, there are lots of words, many of them seven- and eight-letter words, that begin and end with an **S**. Then there are armies of words ending in –**ISES** and –**ISTS**. So it's far from impossible to get a bonus word with two S's. It's just not twice as easy as getting one with one **S**.

Generally, the thing to do with a duplicate **S** is play one, hooking it onto a word already on the board, making another word at the same time, preferably using your higher-scoring other tiles – you should be getting the hang of it by now – and then you're still left with one **S** and your lower-scoring tiles with which, fingers crossed, to get a bonus next time.

S at the beginning

Don't forget that as well as being an 'end hook' (going on the end of a word), the **S** is frequently also a 'front hook'; which, as you've probably worked out, means that it can be placed at the front of a word to form another word. You can often put an **S** at the front of words beginning with:

C: **(S)CAM, (S)CAMP, (S)CABBY, (S)CANNER, (S)CURRIED**, and many more, including unusual words like **(S)CAMEL** and **(S)COPULATE**.

H: **(S)HOD, (S)HALL, (S)HATTER, (S)HEATH, (S)HELLFIRE**, and did you know **(S)HADDOCK** and **(S)HOOKS**?

L: **(S)LAP, (S)LINK, (S)LOUGH, (S)LIPPY, (S)LIGHTLY**, and nice words like **(S)LOWDOWN** and **(S)LAUGHTER**.

P: **(S)PUD, (S)PRAY, (S)PRINT, (S)PRIEST, (S)PLATTER**, and the more unexpected **(S)PINK** and **(S)PROD**.

T: **(S)TRAP, (S)TANNIC, (S)TICKER, (S)TAKEOUT**, and **TATUS**, the plural of an old spelling of **tattoo**, converts rather pleasingly into **STATUS**.

Words beginning with **M, N, W**, and even **Q** are also good to check for **S** front-hooks. And of course, like most other consonants, it will often go before a word starting with a vowel (**SADDER, SEVEN, SIRE, SODIUM, SUNDRESS**). Add in exotica like **SDEIGN** and **SGRAFFITI** and you might almost start to think an **S** was as likely to go before a word as after it. But it is its power as an end hook that makes the **S** such a potent weapon to have on your rack.

good to know

Some unexpected words that take S (i.e. can have an S put at the end of them):
EROTIC
ERRATIC
MALTED
PRY
TELLY
TRILBY
WICKED

Using the blank

Sometimes a very inexperienced player will feel hard done by when they pick the blank, because it doesn't score anything. *Wrong, wrong, wrong!*

If you pick a blank, your heart should leap like a March hare on a trampoline. So long as there is an opening on the board somewhere, a blank should set you on your way to being able to play a bonus word; maybe not immediately, but reasonably soon.

Why? It's those combinations again. The larger the number of different ways you can form your rack into seven letters, the more likely it is that one of them will be a seven-letter word. We've already noted that a straightforward rack of seven different letters can be arranged 5,040 different ways. But six different letters *plus a blank* can be arranged in a massive 115,920 ways, counting the blank as each possible letter in each separate position. That's twenty-three times as many; picking a blank is like having twenty-three tickets in the lottery instead of just one.

You could try painstakingly working your way through all 115,920 combinations to find if you have a seven-letter word. At, say, ten seconds per combination, that would take about thirteen and a half days, assuming you don't stop for sleeping, eating, or other essentials. Your opponent may get a tad restless.

good to know

Don't forget that the blank has no value, whatever letter it is standing in for.

Happily, your brain will automatically shut out consideration of the vast number of these combinations that are obviously fruitless. You can give the old noddle a helping hand in various ways:

1. If some of your letters form a useful combination such as −**ING** or -**ATE**, put the blank with the other letters and see if any words suggest themselves. **GHILNR**? (? represents a blank) might look a bit of a mishmash. But make it **HLR**? + **ING** and it should immediately resolve itself into **HURLING**.

2. If there are no such handy combinations on your rack, go through the alphabet, making the blank each letter in turn. **DFIMNU**? may not immediately look like anything, but once you try making the blank an **L**, **MINDFUL** might pop into your head.

3. Perhaps the blank will become the last letter in one of those useful combinations. **GHILRU**? also makes **HURLING**, even though you can't immediately isolate −**ING**.

4. You may be able to save a bit of time and mental energy by eliminating several possibilities for the blank. For instance, if you have five consonants, one vowel, and a blank, the blank is almost certainly going to have to be a vowel if you are using it to make a seven-letter word. Even more obviously, with five bonus-friendly tiles (i.e. mainly one-pointers with a good vowel-consonant balance) plus a blank and a **Q**, there's really only one letter you need to think about making the blank. If you don't have a **U**, that's almost certainly what the blank is going to have to be

if you are going for a bonus.

You must avoid the ultimate Scrabble crime of wasting your blank for a low score. Don't just stick it into a four- or five-letter word for a few points, even if you can't see anything else. Hold onto the blank and get rid of some of your more awkward tiles, even for a lower score this time round, and some bonus possibilities ought to start revealing themselves within one or two moves.

In club and tournament Scrabble, the blank will rarely be played other than in a bonus move, unless the blank is picked right at the end of the game, when it may be too late to knock the rest of the rack into shape or there may be nowhere to play a bonus.

You may also be able to use the blank to get a move as good as a bonus, even if not an actual one. Remember we talked about getting a **J**, **Q**, **X**, or **Z** on a Premium Letter Square, at the same time as getting the word on a Premium Word Square. That can easily score sixty to seventy points or more, and could be well worth using a blank for.

As a general rule, you should be looking to score at least twenty for an **S**, preferably more than twenty-five, and at least fifty for a blank.

Two blanks

Even some quite experienced club players claim to dislike getting two blanks at the same time. The mesmerisingly high number of different combinations they can make throws some people

good to know

Do you ever feel the blank in the Scrabble bag? Mattel produce special tile sets for tournaments where every tile is smooth.

into confusion, and they say they 'just can't think', or even, appropriately enough, 'go blank'.

This is a bit like people who say that being rich doesn't make you happy. It may be true, but you wouldn't mind giving it a try anyway.

The fact is that with two blanks you should be well on your way to making a bonus, unless the board is extremely blocked. If you find a double blank difficult to cope with, try thinking of one of them as the most useful letter it could be (bearing in mind your other five tiles) if it was not a blank. With a rack of, say, **AACIP**??, given that you have three vowels, at least one of your blanks is going to be a consonant. So think of it as one of those one-point, bonus-friendly consonants like **N** or **T**, and words like **CAPTAIN** and **CAPITAL** should soon start suggesting themselves to you. If you have **HORTX**??, make the rack more manageable by calling one blank an **E**, and **EXHORTS** suddenly becomes much easier to find.

Having said that, playing an **X** and two blanks in one word is being a bit like the kid at the party who eats her cake, jelly and ice-cream all at once. And we know how she's going to feel in twenty minutes. With a rack like that, you may be able to play your **X**, perhaps with one of the blanks, for forty-odd points, and still have a good chance of the bonus next turn. Unless you can play **EXHORTS** (or whatever) for a real stonker of a score – I would suggest at least eighty – a rack with lots of goodies like that should be good for two high scores.

Above all, *never change a blank*. Why give your opponent the chance of picking it later? The only possible time you might want to try breaking that rule is if you are over a hundred behind, and thus need two bonuses to come back. You could try putting a blank back in the hope of picking it later and getting bonuses with both of them. But this is a tactic you will use rarely if ever – particularly as by changing you waste a shot and fall even further behind.

HAVE A GO

CHALLENGE NO. 4

Your rack: **B D O R R S ?**

What type of letter is the blank almost certainly going to be to form a seven-letter word?

Can you find the seven-letter word? And where would you play it?

6 Finding the bonus words

Once you have mastered (and I do mean mastered) the twos, started learning some useful threes, lost your fear of the **JQXZ**, and realized the value of the S and the blank, the next step on your road to being an accomplished Scrabble player is to be able to play bonus words; in other words, play out all seven of your letters in one go for that lovely, satisfying, game-changing, onlooker-impressing, opponent-shattering fifty-point bonus.

Making bonus words

You may manage the occasional bonus now, but if you can get up to playing a regular one per game, then two per game, you will soon see your average score rocketing out of the sub-200 doldrums and into the stratosphere of 300+ and even 400+ (based on a two-player game).

So how is it done? Essentially, there are two keys to playing bonuses regularly: **knowing the words** and **managing your rack**. Let's look at the second one first.

Managing your rack

1. Keeping the right letters.
As we have now said several times, it's not just knowing words, it's knowing the right words that counts. There is no point at all in indulging in an orgy of random seven-letter-word learning. **PUPUNHA**, **MUNDIFY**, or **THRUTCH** may just show up on someone's rack somewhere between now and the next millennium, but that's not the way to bet. Better by far to get familiar with words which, on the balance of probabilities, will come up on your rack with reasonable regularity.

Rack management essentially means knowing which letters to keep and which letters to get rid of to maximize your chances of a good score next time – preferably a bonus. Just as a good snooker player doesn't take a whack at the first ball he sees but tries to make sure he leaves himself an easy shot for next time, so should a Scrabble player have an eye to what he or she is storing up for the future. Perhaps it's no surprise Messrs Davis and Wattana are such mean operators around the Scrabble board.

The first thing to know when it comes to working out which letters to keep and which to play is the distribution of the tiles in a set. In other words, how many A's are there, how many B's, etc. Happily, many Scrabble boards actually list this distribution down one side of the board. If yours doesn't, it's fairly easy to have a rough idea of how many of a particular letter are in the set by its point value:

POINT VALUE	NUMBER IN SET
1	4-12
2	3-4
3-4	2
5-10	1

Clearly, the fewer points a letter scores, the more there are of them. This makes sense. You get lots of the common letters to help you make words, but they don't score so much. There are fewer of the less common letters because they're harder to use, but they are worth more points.

So we can see that, other things being equal, our rack is going to tend towards having a lot of the one-point tiles. Sixty-eight of the ninety-eight tiles (leaving aside the blanks) are worth one point. So the best bonus words to learn must be the ones consisting wholly or mainly of one-point tiles.

So which are the one-point letters? There are ten of them: the five vowels **AEIOU**, plus five consonants, **LNRST**.

But are these the ten commonest letters in the language? A statistical analysis of over a million words of English covering newspaper reports, scientific and religious writing, and general fiction, computed that the most frequently used letters, in order, were:

E T A O I N S R H L

So nine of our ten commonest letters in the Scrabble set agree with those brought out by this study. The rogue interloper is **H**, but its frequency can be explained by the number of short, very common words in which it appears: **THE, THAT, THIS, THESE, THOSE, HE, SHE, THEY, HIM, HER, THEM, HIS, HERS, THEIR, WHICH, WHAT, WHO, HOW, WHY**.

Thus the letter **H** would appear in a passage of written or spoken English much more often than it would in a random collection of unconnected words.

So the missing letter from our 'Scrabble Top Ten', the **U**, presumably came eleventh in the statistical survey? Actually, it came thirteenth, behind **D** and **C**.

So why are there so many **U**'s in the Scrabble set? Scrabble legend has it that Alfred Butts decided on the number of each letter by counting the frequency with which each appeared in the leader page of one issue of the *New York Times*. But it seems clear that he must have made some judicious adjustments after his mammoth count. He would have had to iron out the **H** problem, for one. And he also realized that there had to be a reasonable number of **U**'s so that players could play the **Q**. (**QI**, **QAT**, **QADI** and the rest of them would not have been part of his thinking at that time.) Four **U**'s would have been enough to give a reasonable chance of shedding the awkward **Q**, but not so many that players would be overburdened with a letter which, apart from **Q** duty, is not particularly helpful.

2. The right vowels.
The vowels have a fairly clear hierarchy of usefulness. **E** is the biggie. It's difficult (far from impossible, but difficult) to get a bonus without an **E**. As you may have discovered yourself, it can be hard playing any good move at all without an **E**. **A** and **I** come next, about equally useful, closely followed by **O**. As the ideal vowel-consonant split is three vowels and four consonants, it would seem to follow that the vowels you want on your rack are **AEI**. Even though our million-word analysis placed **O** above **I**, experience in Scrabble shows that the **I** is easier to work with – lots of nice suffixes like –**ING**, –**IER**, –**IEST**, –**ISE**, –**IZE**, –**ISM** and –**IST**.

So you try to keep **AEI** on your rack if you get them, and play any **O** or **U** that you have? Maybe, but it's not always quite that simple.

The problem of duplicated letters can easily come to haunt you with vowels, especially the **A** and **I**. You don't want two of either of these letters on your rack, because comparatively few words have two **A**'s or two **I**'s in them. Yes, there are all the words ending in –**ING**, thus giving **AIMING**, **BOILING**, **CHIDING**, and lots of others, or the **-IER** and **-IEST** words – **DIRTIER**, **FIERIER**, **GIDDIEST**, etc, and no doubt you can rattle off a dozen words off the top of your head with two **A**'s as well, but the fact is that duplicates radically diminish the number of different ways you can arrange the letters on your rack, and that constricts the number of useful moves you can make.

For this reason, it is always a good idea to keep track of how many **A**'s and **I**'s have been played. Let's say it's about halfway through the game, with about forty-five or fifty letters on the board. There are six **A**'s on the board and two **I**'s. You also have one of each on your rack. You can see that you are far more likely to pick in another I than another **A**, so it makes sense to play the I if you can, but not be so concerned about ditching the **A**.

This should not take precedence over any really good move you can make that involves keeping the **I** and playing the **A**. But, other things being equal, play the **I**. A choice between **BAD** and **BID**? Go for **BID**. Wondering about **CARP**? Perhaps with a judicious reshuffle you could make it **PRIG** instead.

If you play bridge or poker, you will know the value of remembering the cards that have been played or folded. In poker, you don't try for the third six to go with your pair if both the other sixes are gone. In bridge, the king of trumps must win a trick if the ace is gone. We are using the exact same principle here in Scrabble. You use your knowledge of what has already been played to help you predict what will happen next. Except it's easier in Scrabble because you don't need to remember – the 'discarded' letters are all there face up on the board in front of you, so all you need to do is count them. (You might not even need to do that – in a later chapter, we'll look at the concept of **tile-tracking**, which shows you at a glance how many of each letter are still to come.)

The **E**, as we have already seen, is a sufficiently useful letter that to hold two of them is no bad thing. And there are plenty of four-letter words with a double **O** in the middle if you want to get rid of a couple of **O**'s – but four-letter words with two **A**'s or two **I**'s are considerably thinner on the ground, as you will discover if you try to think of some. Of course, you don't need to get rid of *both* your duplicates to alleviate your problem, you only need to play one – but there is a comfort in having those double-**O** words available if you need them.

So, we have the apparently contradictory situation that one **A** or one **I** on your rack is better than one **O**, because **A** and **I** are commoner letters, especially for bonuses. But two **O**'s are better than two **A**'s or two **I**'s, bcause they're easier to get rid of in short words. So it's halfway through a game, there are four **A**'s, four **I**'s and four **O**'s to come, and you have one of each on your rack. Do you play **BID**, **BAD**, or **BOD**?

The answer is, *probably*, play **BOD**. The extra strength of **A** and **I** over **O** just about overrides the fear of picking a duplicate. But much would depend on other factors. For example, if you have **TION** on your rack, is it worth holding this useful suffix and playing the **A**? It could be, but you need to be aware that –**TION** is mainly useful for eight-letter bonuses; there are not many seven-letter words ending in –**TION**. So don't build your hopes up of getting a –**TION** bonus unless there are places on the board where an eight-letter word is playable.

If you think this is all starting to sound a bit technical, well, you're right. But that's the trouble with Scrabble racks – there is not always a clear-cut answer. It's like walking through a wood. This path is more overgrown, that one is muddier, a third goes uphill, and the fourth one looks pretty but there's a strange growling noise coming from its vicinity. Which one do you take? Hitting on the right one is a mixture of experience, common sense, instinct, and luck.

Anyway, we have established that, inasmuch as we can generalize, **E** is the best vowel, **A** and **I** come next, **O** a little behind but with some points in its favour, and **U** the least useful. But even the humble **U** can be worth hanging onto if it is towards the end of the game and the **Q** hasn't appeared yet, especially if there are no handy places to slot in a **QI** or a **QAT**.

So in fact, the distribution of vowels in a set – twelve **E**'s, nine **A**'s, nine **I**'s, eight **O**'s, and four **U**'s – turns out to be about right. Well done, Alfred Butts and the *New York Times*.

3. The right consonants.

So what about consonants? Remember which are the one-point tiles –**LNRST**. Holding on to these and discarding the rest is generally the quickest way to a bonus word. But as always, there are complications.

Of these five consonants, **L** is unquestionably the least useful. It should really be worth one and a half points. Hang on to it if you like but have no qualms about playing it away if you have a good move in which to play it.

The **S** is a special case which we have already discussed. If your rack is your afternoon tea-break, the S is a cream cake – great to have, but two are no better than one and might leave you feeling sick.

The **N** is a common letter and is useful for forming words with –**ING**, –**TION**, and –**SION**. But a word of warning about the **N** – it's a terrible letter for beginning words with. Try this little experiment: take your dictionary or Scrabble word book, and hold the 'N' section between your thumb and forefinger. Look how skimpy it is. There are more words beginning with **W** than beginning with **N**. I ask you – **W**. A rubbishy letter that Alf Butts saw fit to give us only two of, and frankly that's probably too many. But you can start more words with it than you can with an **N**. So if you have an **N** in the left-hand column, and you're trying to use it to start an eight-letter word for a bonus, my advice is – try something else, fast.

Now, how about the **R**? Another useful letter, but again there's a catch. The **R** really needs an **E** to give it much value. It comes into its own because of the large number of words with the prefix **RE**–, or the suffix –**ER** (whether in its agent noun sense, e.g. **COUNTER**, **BUILDER**, or as a comparative of an adjective, e.g. **BLACKER**, **NEEDIER**). And it will not have escaped your notice that the one letter in both **RE**– and –**ER**, apart from **R**, is **E**. So if you don't have an **E**, and there aren't so many left that you're likely to pick one in any time soon, don't bust a gut to hold on to an **R**.

Which leaves the **T**. I am a **T** fan – apart from a blank, **S**, or **E**, no letter gives me more comfort to hold on my rack than a **T**. The only trouble is, the statistics don't back up my enthusiasm as far as seven- and eight-letter words are concerned – the **N** and the **R** are slightly better, because of all those **-ING**s, **RE**-s, and **-ER**s. But that may be the point – the **T** is not dependent on specific other letters to make it useful, and my gut feeling is that its versatility makes it more valuable. A duplicate **T** is also far less of a handicap than a duplicate **N** or **R**. Cherish your **T**'s, try not to play them unless you have no reasonable alternative, and a fair percentage of them will help you on the way to that elusive bonus.

I could analyse my games and try to produce statistics to back this up, but the trouble is that it would be something of a self-fulfilling prophecy. If I (generally) hold onto a **T** until I can make a bonus word with it, then I will obviously be able to count my bonuses and announce triumphantly that fifty percent of them (or whatever) have a **T** in them, which wouldn't prove anything. But the **T** is a cheerful, sociable letter that will fit in with pretty much any rack it finds itself on, so if it knocks on your door, invite it in and make it comfortable. More often than not, it will reward your hospitality.

4. The right balance.
It goes without saying that if you've got a rack of **LNRSSTT**, or **AEEIOOU**, then you haven't got a bonus. In fact, you haven't got any much of a move at all. It's essential to maintain a balance of vowels and consonants.

Let's say your opponent has started the game with **CLOT**, and your rack is as shown:

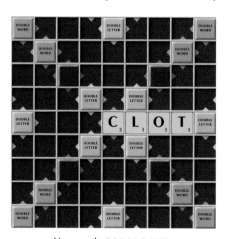

Your rack: **F I L N O U W**

Your first thought might be to play **FLOWN** through the **O**. That would get the high-scoring **F** on a Triple Letter Square and net you an acceptable twenty-one. But look what you've left yourself with on your rack: **IOU**. You may well pick at least two vowels among your four replacement tiles, leaving you with a vowel-heavy rack and little hope of a decent score next time.

You could still play **FLOWN**, but using the **L** on the board rather than the **O**. That only gets you sixteen points, but leaves you with a more acceptable **ILU**. Still a bit too vowelly – ideally, if playing four tiles, you want to leave yourself two consonants and a vowel. The golden rule is that, where possible, you should leave yourself with either the same number of vowels as consonants, or one or two more consonants than vowels.

FLOUT, using the **T**, would give us the desired two-consonants-one-vowel outcome, and also scores sixteen. The main disadvantage of **FLOUT** is that **O** next to the Triple Letter Square; although you have to play your own game and not worry too much about what your opponent might have, on this occasion the pesky blighter only needs a **Z** and an **O** up his or her sleeve to score sixty-five points, leaving you with a disheartening deficit at this stage of proceedings.

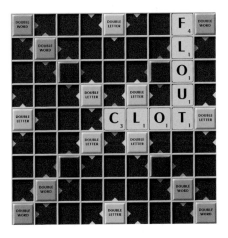

Remembering that we should also be trying for **parallel** rather than **crosswise** plays, we might try **FOWL**, like so:

Not bad. Eighteen points, though we're back to leaving ourselves with two vowels and one consonant. Pity about the L on the Double Letter Score, rather than a higher-scoring letter. Hang on – how about **WOLF** in the same position? Now we've got our score up to twenty-one, the same as if we'd played **FLOWN**, and a more acceptable leave of **INU**. (Scrabble players refer to the letters left on their rack after a move as the 'leave'.)

As so often in Scrabble, there is no clear-cut answer. **WOLF** and **FLOUT** both have something to recommend them, and personally I would go for **WOLF**. But they're both a big improvement on **FLOWN**, because of the better leave – we have given ourselves a better chance of a *balanced rack* for our next move.

5. Keep letters that go together.
It's not just a case of keeping **NRST** and **AEI** and maintaining a good vowel-balance ratio. Often you'll have to keep some other letters as well – you may not have many of **AEINRST**, so you have to decide what else to offload. Again, much will depend on what good scores are available – never lose sight of the fact that that is the object of the exercise. But it will often be worth accepting a less than optimal score to give yourself that all-important optimal leave. If you have a rack **CDGKW** and two vowels, you don't

want to leave yourself with incompatible letters like **GKW**, which are unlikely to combine together in a profitable way next time. Far better to play **GW**, probably along with a vowel, and leave yourself with **CDK**, a much happier combination, especially if you draw (or already have) an E to go with them.

Some Scrabble players refer to a combination like **CDK** as having better *synergy* than one like **GKW**, although others just say that the letters go together, which is every bit as good.

Prefixes and Suffixes

So you're holding on to a reasonable balance of vowels and consonants. You're keeping the letters **NRST** and **AEI** (think of the word **RETAINS**) when you can, as long as you are scoring reasonably in the meantime. When you keep other letters, you are trying to make sure they are compatible with each other. But the seven-letter words are unlikely to just turn up on your rack with all the letters in the right order. You still have to sort the letters out.

So how do you find the seven-letter word that may be sitting on your rack, begging to be played and earn you those fifty lovely bonus points?

The first things to check for are **prefixes and suffixes**. We have touched on these already – suffixes such as –**ING**, –**ED**, –**ISE** (or –**IZE** if you're holding the **Z**), –**ER** and –**EST** (especially –**IER** and –**IEST**), –**ISH**, –**ABLE**, –**AGE**, –**ATE**, –**ANT**, –**ENT**, –**IST**, –**MAN** and –**MEN**, –**LESS**, –**NESS**, –**LIKE**, –**TION**, and –**LY**.

Remember that some of these suffixes can do a double duty. –**ER** can form an *agent noun* (**BUILDER** from **BUILD**), or a *comparative adjective* (**SHORTER** from **SHORT**). –**ISH** can go after an adjective or noun to mean 'somewhat' or 'somewhat like' (**WARMISH**, **HAWKISH**) but, if you have an **F**, you could also try and catch one of the many available **FISH** which may be swimming around, such as **CATFISH**, **DOGFISH**, or the rather unimaginatively-named **FINFISH**.

A quick word of warning about –**ING**. It's very tempting to hang onto these letters if you get them, come what may, in the expectation that they are bound to combine with almost any other four letters to form a seven-letter word. Well, sometimes they will and sometimes they won't, but it doesn't happen as often as you might think. In the meantime you are effectively trying to play with only your other four letters, drastically minimizing your potential score. And if and when you do get an −**ING** word, the double-consonant −**NG** can make it difficult to fit into a parallel play, so you may well not be able to get it down on the board.

One of the most difficult things in Scrabble is when you *know* you're close to a seven-letter bonus but you haven't quite got one (or can't quite find it if you have). You are loath to play more than one or two of your tiles, because you don't want to break up your promising combination of −**ERING** or −**NIEST** or what have you. But that means you are scoring only a handful of points, while your opponent may be forging ahead with twenties and thirties. After three attempts, you may finally get your bonus for, say, sixty-five points, only to find that while you were faffing around scoring six or eight at a time, your opponent notched up seventy-five points altogether and you are no better off.

So what are we saying here? Do you or don't you hang onto a **RETAINS** combination like **AENT**, or a suffix like −**ISH**? Do you just check to see if they can help you make a seven-letter word if you have them on your rack at the time, but if they don't just play what you can for a decent score? Or do you hoard them, in the hope that next shot you will be able to put down that satisfying, opponent-demoralizing bonus?

There is no easy answer. Among the things to take into account are:

1. **The score**.
   If you are appreciably behind, you may have no alternative but to go for a bonus. If you're ahead, try to keep your score moving along and don't worry so much about bonus-hunting.

2. **The state of the board**.
   Are there places to play a bonus word if you do get one?

3. **Are there bonus letters left to come?**
   There is little point in trying for a bonus if the unseen letters are mainly **O**'s, **U**'s, and higher-scoring consonants.

Well. A quick warning about not getting too obsessed with hanging onto –**ING** has become an angst-ridden treatise about whether it's worth going for bonuses at all. But the extra fifty gives you such a powerful propulsion of points that it is worth devoting a lot of time to learning how to get them. If your rack is even starting to look as if it might make a bonus, and the board has openings or spaces where you can create openings, then it has to be worth considering.

Having talked about suffixes, we mustn't forget about their handy little counterparts, the prefixes. The kings of the prefix world are **RE**- and **UN**-. A quick glance through the **RE**- and **UN**- sections of *Collins Scrabble Words* makes it seem as if you can put either of these two little pairs of letters before almost any word at all. You will quickly be disabused of this notion if you start trying to do so during a game. There are many, many words, some of which look perfectly reasonable, that cannot be formed in this way.
You **CANNOT** play:

> **RECLAMP**　　**RECOACH**　　**RESLUMP**　　**RESTAND**　　**RETRICK**

any of which look as feasible as some words which are valid, such as **REVICTUAL**, **RESPLICE**, and **REEDIFY** (hyphen not compulsory).
Likewise, *Collins Scrabble Words* does **NOT** give the nod of approval to:

> **UNLIGHT**　　**UNDARK**　　**UNRUNG**　　**UNHAIRY**　　**UNSAD**

If **UNHAPPY**, why not **UNSAD**? And if **UNHEARSE**, **UNHONEST**, and **UNMELLOW**, all of which are allowed, why not **UNLIGHT** or **UNHAIRY**?

Remember, Scrabble players didn't write *Collins Scrabble Words*, lexicographers did. And they will generally say that they can cite an example of usage for all the words in their dictionary, and have excluded those for which they could not find such a usage. Fine, but it doesn't help you much when you're trying to work out whether to risk

REHAPPEN or **UNSEXY**. (The latter is valid, the former not.)

So **UN-** and **RE-** are useful to remember, and well worth putting to one side of your rack to see whether they'll help you towards a bonus, but the frequency with which they can be used makes it all the more heartbreaking when, like a wayward lover, a broken-down car, or a snapped piece of elastic, they let you down when you need them most.

There are lots of other common prefixes which can ease your path towards that elusive seven-letter word. Watch out for

PRE-	PRO-	ANTI-	DIS-	MIS-	OUT-	OVER-
DE-	EN-	IN-	CON-	SUB-	and	UP-

Apart from prefixes and suffixes, how else can we discover seven-letter words on our rack? We have covered the obvious one of **words ending in S**. If you have an **S**, always pop it to the end of your rack, and see if your other six letters can make a six-letter word that your **S** might go on the end of to make a seven.

Compound words

Something else to watch for is **compound words**. This can often pay dividends even if you have higher-scoring letters on your rack. Does your rack divide into a three-letter word and a four-letter word? If so, they just might combine to form a seven. There are lots of examples:

PAYBACK	**AIRLINE**	**MANHUNT**	**FOOTPAD**	**SEAFOOD**
REDCOAT	**SUNTRAP**	**WARSHIP**	**HATBAND**	**KEYHOLE**

All these techniques may of course lead you to an eight-letter word (using a letter on the board) and this method in particular can lead you to a 4-4, 3-5, or 5-3 compound word:

AIRTIGHT	**WORMWOOD**	**BLUEBIRD**	**PAYCHECK**	**CAUSEWAY**

Always look at your letters in as many different ways as you can. A word with a **Q** doesn't have to **begin** with a **Q**. Words can begin with vowels, or end with vowels other than **E**.

Try and unravel these twenty teasers. Five take unexpected letters before them to form other words. Five take unexpected letters after them. Five end with **A**, **I**, **O**, or **U**. And five have a **J**, **Q**, **X**, or **Z**, but where it comes in the word is up to you to discover. Some will be compound words or will use affixes.

When you've got them, work out which ten have the unexpected 'hooks' – and see if you can find them. For example, if the answer was **BRIDGES**, the hook would be **ABRIDGES**. Or for a hook at the end, **ELEVATOR** would become **ELEVATORY** (as well as

good to know

Some three-and four-letter words are particularly good for creating compound words, such as AIR, SEA, SHIP, MAN, MEN, WOOD, WORK, WARD, those FISH again, and some colours such as RED and BLUE.

the obvious **ELEVATORS**).

SIPRAIN	RAJTHING	CANTHEN	AIMSTRAP	QUARPET
THRIVEON	FLYWAUL	SHEISVAL	FILMNAG	IPLOTSEX
AIHOOTS	DRAWPLOY	AACEHUT	RUEPHONE	ZELEGAL
PLUMTILE	IMAPLOD	HATEDEER	ILOVAIR	ZREFEREE

Answers

ASPIRIN (ASPIRING) NIGHTJAR ENCHANT (PENCHANT) PASTRAMI PARQUET OVERTHIN (OVERTHINK) AWFULLY (LAWFULLY) LAVISHES (LAVISHEST) FLAMING (FLAMINGO) EXPLOITS ATISHOO WORDPLAY (SWORDPLAY) CHATEAU HEREUPON (THEREUPON /WHEREUPON) GAZELLE MULTIPLE (MULTIPLEX) DIPLOMA REHEATED (PREHEATED) RAVIOLI REFEREEZE

Note that as well as **X** and the obvious **S**, **MULTIPLE** also takes a **T**, a multiplet being a term from optics. And of course some of the other words have hooks as well, such as **CHATEAUX** and **DIPLOMAT**.

The only other advice I can give in spotting bonus words is simply to look for them. Obvious, I know – but it's easy to get into the habit of playing that reasonable move for twenty points or so, or that word which will leave you a perfectly-balanced and compatible rack, while all the time the seven-letter word is hiding in there somewhere. The more you play, the more you will develop a feel for whether a rack is likely to contain a bonus.

Have a look at these racks and, without at first trying to work out what the seven-letter words might be, decide which combinations are likely to make a seven-letter word.

Then when you've done that, try and figure out the words:

> **ACDEHIR**   **ABINOPT**   **AELMNSV**   **EEFGLOR**   **AEINOST**

Let's look at them one at a time. **ACDEHIR** seems to have possibilities. The **C** and **H** might go together. And there's an **RE/ER**, in fact an **IER**, with other possibilities like **ED** and **IC**. **CHADIER, DACHIER** – nothing there. **CHAIDER, REDAICH** – the **RE** and **ER** don't appear to be much help. Maybe **IC** at the end – **HERADIC**? No, but a usable **L** on the board would give **HERALDIC**. A compound, perhaps – **ICEHARD, HARDICE**? **ICEHARD** sounds feasibly poetic but you haven't actually seen it anywhere, so it's a big risk. Finally, with the simple expedient of trying **ED** at the end to see if there might be a nice, simple past tense, and keeping our compatible **CH** together, we find the answer – **CHAIRED**.

Now for **ABINOPT**. There is a **TION** in there but the only way the other three letters might go with them is **BAPTION** – not a word. No compounds suggest themselves, nothing ending with **ANT**. The **ANTI** prefix likewise leads nowhere, unless someone who doesn't like dancing could be **ANTIBOP** – which is getting into the realms of fantasy. **BIOPTAN** sounds vaguely scientific but that doesn't make it a word. Finally, we correctly conclude that there is no seven-letter word here.

How about **AELMNSV**? Like **ABINOPT**, it has five one-point tiles. It has an **S**, and both **MAN** and **MEN**. Any six-letter words from **AELMNV** that the **S** might go after? **MALVEN, VELMAN, MENVAL** – all rubbish. **ELSV** doesn't combine with **MAN**, nor **ALSV** with **MEN**. The **AELMNS** make a nice start and would go with various other letters to form a seven, but the **V** fouls things up – once again, regretfully, no seven-letter word.

On to **EEFGLOR**. Not too promising on the face of it. **EFGLO** don't match up with **RE** or **ER** – **GEFOLER, REFLOGE**? Not a chance. **GOLFER** is in there but we have an **E** left over – still, it could be worth playing if we can get it on at least a Double Word for twenty or so. Any compounds? **EELFROG? LOGFREE? FOREGEL?** Hang on – **FORELEG**.

The 4-3 split, using the fairly common **FORE** prefix, brings us to the promised land of the seven-letter word. We got there mainly by technique, but with just that last little mental jump to finish the job. As Edison said, 99 per cent perspiration, 1 per cent inspiration. Actually, old Thomas might have been a pretty nifty Scrabble player, but not until after he'd invented the light bulb so that we could see to play in the dark winter evenings.

So how about **AEINOST**? Now this looks good. Six of our **RETAINS** letters, and the seventh is a fairly acceptable **O**. A slight excess of vowels, but we have an **S** and there are prefixes and suffixes galore – -(I)EST, -ATE, -ISE, -TION, -SION, IN-, EN-, ANTI-. So what's the word?

Well, there is one, but you could probably shuffle your tiles till they crumble to dust between your fingers and you wouldn't find it. It's **ATONIES**, which means lack of muscle tone. Or more exactly, it's the plural of **ATONY**, which means lack of muscle tone, so **ATONIES** are more than one lack of muscle tone. It's an awkward, obscure word which not one person in a hundred will come across outside the confines of a Scrabble board. But **ATONY** is in the source dictionary, so it's in *Collins Scrabble Words*, and since the rule used in compiling *Collins Scrabble Words* is that all nouns have a plural, that means **ATONIES** gets in as well.

And that brings us on to one more method of getting bonuses. It might not sound much fun, it might not be your idea of the spirit of a game, but there are many words which will keep coming up on your rack because they are composed of the common letters, and you just have to learn them.

Sometimes games do require a bit of work. Ask a chess player who's memorized fifty standard openings up to the twentieth move. Ask a footballer who's just completed a punishing two-hour training session in a downpour. Ask anyone who's spent hours ringing a premium rate phone line or gone to countless auditions trying to get on *Who Wants To Be a Millionaire* or *The Weakest Link*.

So the next chapter will cut through the tips, techniques, and strategies, and quite simply give you a whole batch of seven- and eight-letter words which, if you can learn them, will help you play bonus after bonus and really get your game moving up through the gears. You won't learn them all today, or tomorrow, but make a start, and come back to them as often as you can and learn a few more. You learnt the twos (or I hope you did) and some of the threes – you may well find sevens and eights easier because the words have a more familiar structure and may just seem less unlikely. It's a bit of a blow to the ego to be told there are so many two- and three-letter words you don't know, but it's easier to accept the existence of these longer words which we have never come across.

The words are divided into logical groups, and the lists are not exhaustive; many others could have been included, but at this stage you would be wise to concentrate on a manageable number. When a combination of seven or eight letters makes more than one word, these are sometimes shown, but not always. Even when more than one word is shown, there may be others with the same letters. But what is there is plenty to be getting on with. So make yourself a nice cup of tea, get your brain in gear, and turn over.

need to know

It's rarely worth worrying about hyphens with bonus words. Words like REEJECT, CODRIVE, and NONOILY are all valid. North American words are included in *Collins Scrabble Words*, and the hyphen appears to be virtually obsolete in America. Indeed, CODRIVE gives rise to the distinctly odd-looking (to British eyes) CODRIVER – not a river full of cod, but someone who shares the driving.

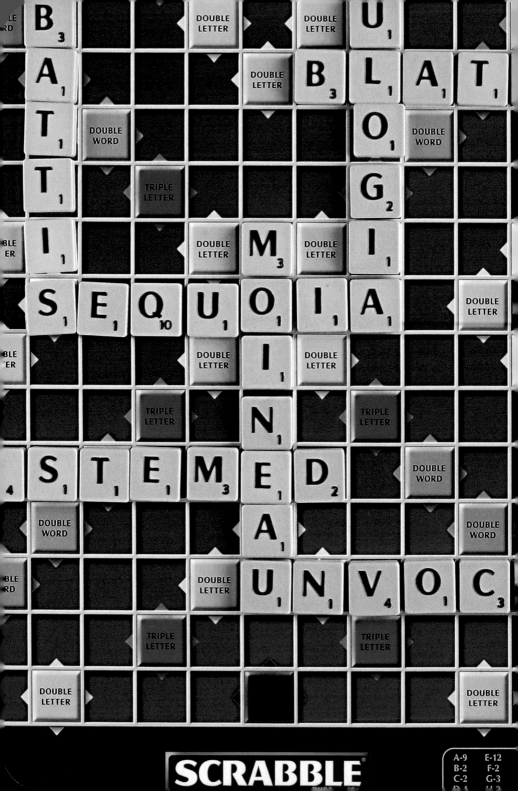

7 Some seven-letter lists

Seven-letter words not only get you bonus
scores, but they also help open up the board.

Seven-letter words

You know by now that, where possible and where it doesn't prevent you from getting a worthwhile score there and then, you are keeping the letters **NRST** and **AEI** to help you towards getting a bonus word.

The letters **AEINRST** alone make several seven-letter words:

RETAINS	**RETINAS**
NASTIER	**STAINER**
RETSINA	**STEARIN**

There are more, but they are rather obscure, and that selection should be enough to enable you to play a bonus on all but the most blocked of boards. The good news is that if you've got any six of the **RETAINS** letters and one other, you've probably got a bonus already. Club players will learn these 'six plus one' lists so that as soon as they have six of the seven, they can mentally flick through the list and come up with the bonus word. It's well worthwhile getting to grips with these lists, so let's set them out here.

Often a combination will make more than one word, but I haven't included every anagram, and a couple of less likely combinations have been excluded. But there are plenty of words for you to get to grips with, and familiarizing yourself with them will dramatically increase the number of bonuses you play.

AEINRS +

C	ARSENIC	CERASIN
D	SANDIER	SARDINE
F	INFARES	SERAFIN
G	SEARING	REGAINS
H	HERNIAS	ARSHINE
I	SENARII	
J	INJERAS	
K	SNAKIER	
L	NAILERS	RENAILS
M	REMAINS	SEMINAR
N	INSANER	INSNARE
O	ERASION	
P	PANIERS	RAPINES
R	SIERRAN	SNARIER
S	SARNIES	ARSINES
T	RETAINS etc.	
V	RAVINES	AVENIRS

AEINRT +

B	ATEBRIN	
C	CERTAIN	NACRITE
D	TRAINED	DETRAIN
E	RETINAE	TRAINEE
F	FAINTER	FENITAR
G	TEARING	GRANITE
H	HAIRNET	INEARTH
I	INERTIA	

AEINRT + *continued*

J	NARTJIE	JANTIER
K	KERATIN	
L	LATRINE	RELIANT
M	MINARET	RAIMENT
N	ENTRAIN	TRANNIE
O	OTARINE	
P	PAINTER	REPAINT
R	TRAINER	RETRAIN
S	RETAINS etc.	
T	NATTIER	NITRATE
U	URINATE	TAURINE
W	TAWNIER	TINWARE

AEINST +

A	ENTASIA	TAENIAS
B	BESAINT	BASINET
C	CANIEST	CINEAST
D	STAINED	INSTEAD
E	ETESIAN	
F	FAINEST	NAIFEST
G	TEASING	INGATES
H	SHEITAN	STHENIA
I	ISATINE	
J	JANTIES	TAJINES
K	INTAKES	TANKIES
L	ENTAILS	SALIENT

AEINST + *continued*

M	INMATES	MAINEST
N	INANEST	STANINE
O	ATONIES	
P	SAPIENT	PANTIES
R	RETAINS etc.	
S	NASTIES	SESTINA
T	INSTATE	SATINET
U	AUNTIES	SINUATE
V	VAINEST	NATIVES
W	TAWNIES	AWNIEST
X	ANTISEX	SEXTAIN
Z	ZANIEST	ZEATINS

AEIRST +

A	ASTERIA	ATRESIA
B	BAITERS	REBAITS
C	RACIEST	STEARIC
D	TIRADES	ASTRIDE
E	AERIEST	SERIATE
F	FAIREST	
G	GAITERS	STAGIER
H	HASTIER	SHERIAT
I	AIRIEST	IRISATE
K	ARKITES	KARITES
L	RETAILS	REALIST
M	MISRATE	SMARTIE

AEIRST + *continued*

N	RETAINS etc.	
O	OARIEST	OTARIES
P	PARTIES	PIRATES
R	TARRIES	ARTSIER
S	SATIRES	TIRASSE
T	ARTISTE	TASTIER
V	VASTIER	TAIVERS
W	WAITERS	WARIEST

AENRST +

A	ANESTRA	
B	BANTERS	
C	CANTERS	TRANCES
D	STANDER	ENDARTS
E	EASTERN	NEAREST
G	STRANGE	GARNETS
H	ANTHERS	THENARS
I	RETAINS etc.	
K	TANKERS	RANKEST
L	RENTALS	ANTLERS
M	SMARTEN	MARTENS
N	TANNERS	
O	SENATOR	TREASON
P	PARENTS	ENTRAPS
R	ERRANTS	RANTERS
S	SARSNET	TRANSES

AENRST + *continued*

T	NATTERS	RATTENS
U	NATURES	SAUNTER
V	SERVANT	TAVERNS
W	WANTERS	STRAWEN
Y	TRAYNES	

AINRST +

A	ARTISAN	TSARINA
B	BRISANT	
C	NARCIST	
D	INDARTS	
E	RETAINS etc.	
G	RATINGS	STARING
H	TARNISH	
L	RATLINS	
M	MARTINS	
N	RATIONS	AROINTS
P	SPIRANT	SPRAINT
Q	QINTARS	
S	STRAINS	INSTARS
T	TRANSIT	STRAINT
U	NUTRIAS	

good to know

Statistically, the seven-letter word you are most likely to pick out of a standard bag of tiles is OTARINE, the adjective from OTARY. An otary is any member of the seal family *with ears*. And what do you call a seal without ears? Anything, it can't hear you.

EINRST +

A	RETAINS etc.	
C	CISTERN	CRETINS
D	TINDERS	
E	ENTRIES	TRENISE
F	SNIFTER	
G	RESTING	STINGER
H	HINTERS	
K	STINKER	TINKERS
L	LINTERS	SNIRTLE
M	MINSTER	ENTRISM
N	INTERNS	TINNERS
O	STONIER	ORIENTS
P	NIPTERS	PTERINS
S	INSERTS	SINTERS
T	TINTERS	ENTRIST
U	UNITERS	NUTSIER
V	INVERTS	STRIVEN
W	WINTERS	TWINERS
Y	SINTERY	

You may have noticed that **AINRST** is by far the shortest of these lists, handicapped as it is by the lack of an E. The **AEINRT** list is not nearly so held back by the absence of an S. **AINRST** does, however, have the saving grace of being the only one to combine with a Q.

Players who are used to dealing with these lists tend to refer to them as the **RETAIN** list, the **SARNIE** list, the **SANTER** list, and so on. Note that SANTER isn't actually a word, it's just a convenient way of referring to the list. 'The **ASTERN** list' doesn't seem to have caught on, for some reason.

There are other lists which are just as good. **RAINED** and **TORIES** are both excellent six-letter combinations for forming sevens:

RAINED +

A	ARANEID	
B	BRAINED	BANDIER
C	CAIRNED	DANCIER
D	DRAINED	DANDIER
F	FRIANDE	
G	READING	GRAINED
H	HANDIER	
I	DENARII	
M	ADERMIN	INARMED
N	NARDINE	
O	ANEROID	
P	PARDINE	
R	DRAINER	RANDIER
S	SARDINE	SANDIER
T	TRAINED	DETRAIN
U	UNAIRED	URANIDE
V	INVADER	RAVINED

TORIES +

A	OARIEST	OTARIES
B	ORBIEST	SORBITE
C	EROTICS	TERCIOS

TORIES + *continued*

D	EDITORS	STEROID
E	EROTISE	
F	FORTIES	FOISTER
G	GOITRES	GORIEST
H	HOISTER	SHORTIE
I	RIOTISE	
K	ROKIEST	
L	LOITERS	TOILERS
M	MOISTER	EROTISM
N	STONIER	ORIENTS
O	SOOTIER	OORIEST
P	RIPOSTE	ROPIEST
R	ROISTER	RIOTERS
S	STORIES	ROSIEST
T	STOITER	
U	TOUSIER	OURIEST
V	TORSIVE	
W	OWRIEST	TOWSIER

There are lots of these 6 + 1 lists that are worth knowing, with the added bonus that once you are familiar with a few, some of the seven-letter words will be known to you already from previous lists. For instance, **RAINED + T** is the same as **RETAIN + D** (**TRAINED, DETRAIN** and the more unusual **ANTIRED**), while **TORIES + N** equals **INTERS + O** (**STONIER, ORIENTS** and a couple of others).

Another way of listing words is by going back to those prefixes and suffixes. It's useful to learn some of the more likely sevens that could come up with each of them. Here are some with the prefixes:

ANTI: ANTIFLU, ANTIFOG, ANTILOG, ANTIPOT, ANTISAG

CON: CONFEST, CONGREE, CONGRUE, CONSEIL, CONURES

DE: DEALATE, DEBRIDE, DEGAMES, DEMEANE, DEPAINT

EN: ENARMED, ENFLAME, ENLIGHT, ENRANKS, ENTAYLE

IN: INDENES, INFAUST, INHUMER, INQUERE, INTURNS

MIS: MISDRAW, MISEDIT, MISKEEP, MISMATE, MISPART

OUT: OUTDARE, OUTEARN, OUTLAND, OUTPORT, OUTWEAR

OVER: OVERAGE, OVERDOG, OVERHOT, OVERMEN, OVERWET

PRE: PREAGED, PRECOOL, PRENAME, PREORAL, PRERACE

PRO: PROETTE, PROLANS, PROLINE, PRONAOS, PROOTIC

SUB: SUBAREA, SUBDEAN, SUBHEAD, SUBLINE, SUBRENT

UP: UPCOILS, UPDRIED, UPLEAPT, UPSTARE, UPTRAIN

There are too many **RE** and **UN** words to list just five, so here is an alphabet of words (nearly) for each one:

REARISE	REINTER	REQUITE
REBREED	REJONES	RERAILS
RECHEAT	REKEYED	RESPELL
REDREAM	RELABEL	RETUNDS
REENDOW	REMERGE	REUNIFY
REFLAGS	RENESTS	REVOTES
REGRATE	REOILED	REWAKEN
REHEARS	REPURES	REZONES

UNALIVE	UNJADED	UNROOTS
UNBARES	UNKINGS	UNSOBER
UNCAPED	UNLEADS	UNTENTY
UNDEALT	UNMITRE	UNURGED
UNEAGER	UNNOBLE	UNVISOR
UNFAIRS	UNOFTEN	UNWATER
UNGIRDS	UNPAINT	UNYOKES
UNHEALS	UNQUIET	UNZONED
UNIDEAL		

Some of the **UN** words in particular are fairly unexpected; it's a bit hard to see how you can **UNWATER** or **UNPAINT** something, and isn't the opposite of **NOBLE**, **IGNOBLE**? It seems from looking at these that you can put **UN** at the front of almost anything, and maybe **RE** as well. *You can't*. It's a hard lesson that all Scrabble players learn sooner or later. Many of these words get into the dictionary through having been used, maybe only once, by a writer – often Shakespeare, who invented a hatful of new words most days before breakfast. Among the

Bard's contributions to the language which we now use as everyday words are *barefaced*, *countless*, *leapfrog*, and *monumental*.

But back to our lists, and where there are prefixes, can suffixes be far behind? Here are some words from those useful suffixes which we looked at previously:

ABLE: CITABLE, FRIABLE, HIDABLE, SEEABLE, TUNABLE

AGE: CORDAGE, LISTAGE, PEONAGE, PIERAGE, SPINAGE

ANT: FLOTANT, ITERANT, PERSANT, REPTANT, SEALANT

ATE: CITRATE, DEALATE, EPILATE, PELTATE, SERIATE

ENT: CONCENT, EXIGENT, FULGENT, MORDENT, PENDENT

IER: BALDIER, HERBIER, LINTIER, RUNTIER, SEDGIER

IEST: AWNIEST, BABIEST, LINIEST, MINIEST, RICIEST

ISE/IZE: ADONISE/IZE, EROTISE/IZE, IRONISE/IZE, POETISE/IZE, RIOTISE/IZE

ISH: ALUMISH, DEAFISH, FLEMISH, MAIDISH, PIGFISH

IST: ABLEIST, DADAIST, ELOGIST, LEFTIST, TUBAIST

LESS: BITLESS, EGOLESS, HATLESS, NAPLESS, TIPLESS

LIKE: BEELIKE, FATLIKE, NETLIKE, RATLIKE, TINLIKE

> *continued*
>
> **LY:** DATEDLY, GAUNTLY, OBESELY, STAIDLY, USEABLY
>
> **MAN/MEN:** BEDEMAN/MEN, GUDEMAN/MEN, LINEMAN/MEN, ODDSMAN/MEN, TOPSMAN/MEN
>
> **NESS:** ALLNESS, FARNESS, HOTNESS, OUTNESS, SHINESS
>
> **TION:** ELUTION, ENATION, LECTION, PACTION, RECTION

It's worth repeating something we said back when we first discussed these prefixes and suffixes (or affixes, as they're collectively known), which is that the four-letter ones often don't make quite as many sevens as you might think. **TION**, for example, is not great for ending seven-letter words. You really need to have scope on the board to make an eight-letter word to get the best out of these slightly longer affixes.

There are too many **-ING** and **-ED** words to make it worth picking out five of each, so here are a few **-ING** sevens that take **S**, which, you remember, means you can put an S at the end of them:

BOLTING(S)	**COOKING(S)**	**DANCING(S)**
FOILING(S)	**GASPING(S)**	**GREYING(S)**
GETTING(S)	**HALTING(S)**	**HOSTING(S)**
KEEPING(S)	**LIMPING(S)**	**NESTING(S)**
PIECING(S)	**RUSTING(S)**	**SEALING(S)**
SEELING(S)	**SHARING(S)**	**STEWING(S)**
TILTING(S)	**WANTING(S)**	

There are a lot of seven-letter words which, while they are termed 'high-probability bonuses', in that they are composed mainly of common letters and are therefore more likely to come up on your rack, they don't fit easily into any of our categories such as containing six of the RETAINS letters, or being formed from a prefix or suffix. Here are some sevens, only a few of which you are likely to be familiar with, but which are well worth knowing, and which we haven't managed to shoehorn into previous lists (or in one or two cases we have, but this list has some anagrams of them). We'll start with some which that four or more vowels, since it's nice to have a few at your fingertips for when you have more vowels than would otherwise be ideal:

Five vowels

AEOLIAN	**ETAERIO**	**OLEARIA**
TAENIAE		

Four vowels (with anagrams grouped together)

ADONISE/ANODISE/SODAINE
AEDILES/DEISEAL
AILERON/ALERION/ALIENOR
AIRDATE/TIARAED

AIRLINE	**ALIENER**	**ALUNITE**
AMNIOTE	**ANEROID**	**ANISOLE**
ANTLIAE	**ARANEID**	**ARENOSE**
ARENOUS	**ATELIER/REALTIE**	
AUDIENT	**AUDILES/DEASIUL**	
DARIOLE	**DEASOIL/ISOLEAD**	

continued

ELATION/TOENAIL	ELOINER	
EMAILED/LIMEADE	EROTICA	GOATIER
GODETIA	INEDITA	
IODATES/TOADIES	ISOLATE	LEIPOAS
LINEATE	MORAINE/ROMAINE	
NIOBATE	OCEANID	ORDINEE
ORIGANE	RADIATE	RAINOUT
REGINAE	ROADIES/SOREDIA	
ROSEATE	TROELIE	URALITE

And here are more than a hundred useful sevens with four and five consonants, likewise grouped into anagrams where appropriate:

AGRISED   AIDLESS/DEASILS

ALBERTS/BLASTER/STABLER

ALBITES/BLASTIE/LIBATES

AMORETS   ANGELIC/ANGLICE

ANGERED/DERANGE/ENRAGED/GRANDEE/
GRENADE

ASTHORE/EARSHOT/HAROSET

ATINGLE/ELATING/GELATIN/GENITAL

BALDIES/DISABLE	BRANSLE	BRANTLE
CANTLES/LANCETS	CARMINE	
CENTERS/CENTRES/TENRECS		CIGARET
CONSTER/CORNETS/CRESTON		
COPIERS/PERSICO		

continued

DESMINE   **DOLINES/INDOLES/SONDELI**

DISCOER

DONSIER/INDORSE/ROSINED

DUNITES   **ESPARTO/PROTEAS/SEAPORT**

ETALONS   **GALORES/GAOLERS**

GENITOR   **GRECIAN**   **HISTONE**

HOGTIES

ISLEMAN/MALINES/MENIALS/SEMINAL

KINGLES   **KINGLET**   **LESBIAN**

LINOCUT   **LINSEED**

LISENTE/SETLINE/TENSILE

MAILERS/REALISM/REMAILS

MANTOES   **MILTERS**

MINERAL/RAILMEN

NAGARIS/SANGRIA/SARANGI

NAMASTE   **NEUTRAL**   **NUTMEAL**

OGREISH   **ONSTAGE**   **ORGANIC**

ORGEATS/STORAGE/TOERAGS

PALSIER/PARLIES   **PAROLES/REPOSAL**

PERIOST/REPOSIT/RIPOSTE/ROPIEST

PERSONA   **PIOLETS/PISTOLE**

SAPROBE   **SEARATS**   **SOLERAS**

STEDING/STINGED   **SYRINGE**   **TELAMON**

TENOURS/TONSURE   **TEOPANS**

TERTIAL   **TONEARM**

Notice how these lists are a mixture of the familiar, like
NEUTRAL, the semi-familiar that you might not think of, like
NUTMEAL and **PERSONA**, and the (almost certainly) unfamiliar,
like **BRANSLE** and **BRANTLE** (variant spellings of an old French

dance), and **SAPROBE** (an organism living in foul water). That's what makes these lists less alarming than they at first appear – you always have a head start with the words you know already.

You know perfectly well what words can be made from **EEDILNS** and **EGINRSY**; it's just a case of getting into your mind that when they appear on your rack you will change them into **LINSEED** and **SYRINGE**. Then in the same way, you will start to recognize the likes of **ACEIMNR** and **EHINOST**. Looking at the letters just sets off that little light-bulb in your head, and, with a bit of practice, it comes to you – **CARMINE**, **HISTONE**, whatever.

A few teasers

Try to find the seven-letter words from these combinations.
They have been graded according to how easy or difficult you
are likely to find them:

1. Almost-**RETAINS** words

11-Plus:	**AEIMNRS**	**EINRSTW**
GCSE Level:	**AEGNRST**	**AENRSTV**
A Level:	**AEIMNRT**	**AINRSTT**
Degree:	**AEHINRT**	**EILNRST**
Doctorate:	**ABEINRT**	**AEHINST**

2. Words with affixes:

Dopy:	**ABEEELS**	**ADILSTY**
Dozy:	**AEIKLRT**	**EINQTUU**
Doughty:	**ABDENSU**	**DEEEKRY**
Deadly:	**ANOOPRS**	**EGILOST**

3. Other useful words:

Clown's car:	**ADEEGNR**	**AEILNOT**
Family car:	**ACGINOR**	**ADEEILM**
Sports car:	**ACEGIRT**	**ADEINOR**
Racing car:	**AEIMNOT**	**CILNOTU**

Answers:

*You can check the answers to Question 1. in the appropriate list
(AEINRS, etc).*

2. *seeable, staidly, ratlike, unquiet, subdean, rekeyed,
pronaos, elogist*

3. *angered (+ anagrams), elation/toenail, organic,
emailed/limeade, cigaret, aneroid, amniote, linocut*

8 Some eight-letter lists

You might not always be able to play a seven-letter word. Here are some tips and lists to help you on your way to playing eight-letter words.

Eight-letter words

Every Scrabble game develops in a slightly different way. Sometimes there are lots of short words played parallel to each other, so the board ends up in an angry little knot of tiles clustered round the centre.

If the words on the outside of this knot are 'blockers' (words which don't take any hooks either at the front or the end), it can get to a stage where it's very difficult to add anything at all.

There isn't likely to be a bonus played here on the next move. It's not impossible – there are eight-letter words ending in U, such as **HAUSFRAU, THANKYOU**, and the rather unlikely **SUCURUJU**, or you might even come up with a nine-letter word using two on the board, like **CHLAMYDIA**, but, realistically, it ain't going to happen.

A slight change to the opening makes all the difference.

A seven-letter word could easily be played on this board, using hooks such as **ITS, ITA, ABA, OBA, LAMA,** or any two-letter word ending in A.

But now consider a completely different kind of beginning.

Memorable anagrams are fun and a great way of getting words to stick. Here are some good eight-letter anagrams:

LAMPPOST/
   PALMTOPS
HANDOUTS/
   THOUSAND
LAKELETS/
   SKELETAL
EPITAPHS/
   HAPPIEST
LICKSPIT/
   LIPSTICK
STEWPANS/
   WASPNEST

But my favourite eight-letter anagram has to be the two words from the letters ABEGMNOY. They are both common 5-3 compound words. Can you get them?

Of course... BOGEYMAN and MONEYBAG.

It looks like a bonus has been played already. It may not – the opening move might have been **QUAKE** or various other words (**WONDER, AKE, DE**, though none of these seem very likely to have produced the board as shown). No matter. The point here is that bonuses are certainly playable onto this board, but probably not a seven. You're going to have to use one of the free letters on the board (a 'floater', in Scrabble jargon) to make an eight-letter word.

There are plenty to choose from: **W, O, N, S, U, A**, and, if you're feeling very clever, **Q** are all plumb in the middle of the board, and if you can combine any of them with the seven on your rack, you will be able to play a bonus. The **D** and the **R** are also possible to use, although they are restricted. And the **K** is just about possible, but hemmed in by other letters.

So what this is leading up to is that, if you want to maximize the number of bonuses you play, you really need to be at home with eights as well as sevens. This chapter will put an army of high-probability eight-letter words at your disposal, all ready for you to slam down on the board for those longed-for fifty bonus points.

Where to start? On the basis that you are still keeping, where it's possible and sensible to do so, those **RETAINS** letters, you could do worse than learn some eights containing those letters – the **RETAINS + 1** list. Of course, a lot of them will be sevens from the **RETAIN** list with an **S** plonked on the end: **DETRAINS, HAIRNETS, MINARETS, TRANNIES**, and many more. There seems little point in listing them – go back to the **RETAIN** list in the previous chapter and try to work them out for yourself.

However, there are a few more which aren't quite

so simple. Here are a few **RETAINS + 1** eights you
might not know, or might not think of so easily:

A	ANTISERA	ARTESIAN	RATANIES
	RESINATA	SEATRAIN	
B	BANISTER	BARNIEST	
C	CANISTER	CARNIEST	CISTERNA
	SCANTIER		
D	RANDIEST	STRAINED	
E	ARSENITE	RESINATE	STEARINE
G	ASTRINGE	GANISTER	GANTRIES
	RANGIEST	STEARING	
I	RAINIEST		
K	NARKIEST		
O	ANOESTRI	ARSONITE	NOTARIES
	ROSINATE	SENORITA	
P	PANTRIES	PINASTER	PRISTANE
R	RESTRAIN	STRAINER	TRANSIRE
S	ARTINESS	SNARIEST	
T	STRAITEN		

Of course, you don't need to have **RETAINS** on
your rack to play these; if you have six of **RETAINS**,
and the seventh is 'floating' on the board, you
effectively have the same thing and may well be able
to play a **RETAINS + 1** word.

It's also handy to know eights you can make from
sets of seven common letters plus one other, when
the seven letters *don't* make a bonus word. Few racks
are more annoying than the ones with good letters
you don't want to break up, but which don't make a
bonus yet. With a rack like **AAEINRT (RETAIN + A)**,

getting a good score can be difficult even playing five or six tiles. Just to play the **A** will probably get you a single-figure score, and while you might get the bonus next time, you might just pick the **Q** or the **X**, or another **A**.

But using a floating letter on the board you can solve the problem by conjuring up an eight, such as:

RETAINA +

B	**RABATINE**	
C	**CARINATE**	**CRANIATE**
D	**DENTARIA**	**RAINDATE**
G	**AERATING**	
M	**ANIMATER**	**MARINATE**
O	**AERATION**	
P	**ANTIRAPE**	
S	See below	
T	**ATTAINER**	**REATTAIN**
U	**INAURATE**	
W	**ANTIWEAR**	
Z	**ATRAZINE**	

It's a bit of an oddity that despite **RETAINA** not making a seven, there are a lot of eights you can make from **RETAINA + S**: you saw them a couple of pages ago in the **RETAINS** + 1 list: **ANTISERA ARTESIAN RATANIES RESINATA SEATRAIN**.

Here are some more eights from good-looking but unproductive sevens:

AEEINRS +

C	CINEREAS	INCREASE
	RESIANCE	
D	ARSENIDE	DENARIES
	DRAISENE	NEARSIDE
G	ANERGIES	GESNERIA
H	INHEARSE	
K	SNEAKIER	
L	ALIENERS	
M	REMANIES	
N	ANSERINE	
P	NAPERIES	
R	REARISEN	
S	SENARIES	
T	ARENITES	ARSENITE
	RESINATE	STEARINE
	TRAINEES	
U	UNEASIER	

AEILORS +

A	OLEARIAS	
C	CALORIES	CARIOLES
D	DARIOLES	SOLIDARE
	SOREDIAL	
F	FORESAIL	

AEILORS + *continued*

G	GASOLIER	GIRASOLE
	SERAGLIO	
H	AIRHOLES	SHOALIER
M	MORALISE	
N	AILERONS	ALERIONS
	ALIENORS	
P	PELORIAS	POLARISE
S	SOLARISE	
T	SOTERIAL	
V	OVERSAIL	VALORISE
	VARIOLES	VOLARIES
Y	ROYALISE	
Z	SOLARIZE	

This list shows that any letter can be useful in the right circumstances; most people hate picking a **V** – perhaps club players more than most, because they know it's the only letter that doesn't make a two-letter word and so are instinctively scared of it. But what do you know – if you're drawing an eighth letter to **AEILORS**, **V** is the best letter of the lot, forming four anagrams.

DEEINRT +

A	DETAINER	RETAINED
B	INTERBED	
D	DENDRITE	
K	TINKERED	

DEEINRT + *continued*

M	REMINTED	
N	INDENTER	INTENDER
	INTERNED	
O	ORIENTED	
R	INTERRED	TRENDIER
S	INSERTED	NERDIEST
	RESIDENT	SINTERED
	TRENDIES	
T	RETINTED	
U	RETINUED	REUNITED
V	INVERTED	
W	WINTERED	
X	DEXTRINE	

You can use your prefixes and suffixes for eights just as much as for sevens – more so, as we have already noted, in the case of some of the four-letter affixes. So here's a selection of useful eights which those by now familiar old friends might lead you to:

ANTI:	ANTIDOTE, ANTIFOAM, ANTIHERO, ANTIMERE, ANTIPORN
CON:	CONGLOBE, CONGREET, CONTANGO, CONTRAIL, CONURBAN
DE:	DEAERATE, DEBRUISE, DEGREASE, DERATTED, DESINING

continued

DIS: DISANNUL, DISCOURE, DISGAVEL, DISLEAVE, DISPLANT

EN: ENCRADLE, ENHALOES, ENLARGEN, ENSAMPLE ENSOULED

IN: INDARTED, INFRUGAL, INNATIVE, INSEEMED, INSTABLE

MIS: MISDREAD, MISGRAFT, MISLEARN, MISPLANT, MISTRACE

OUT: OUTDRESS, OUTHOMER, OUTRANGE, OUTSMILE, OUTWEARY

OVER: OVERDOER, OVERGILT, OVERMELT, OVERSALE, OVERWISE

PRE: PREBLESS, PRECURSE, PRELIMIT, PRERINSE, PRETRIMS

PRO: PROGRADE, PROMETAL, PROSTYLE, PROTONIC, PROVIRAL

SUB: SUBAGENT, SUBCASTE, SUBGENUS, SUBLEASE, SUBTIDAL

UP: UPBEARER, UPGATHER, UPGROWTH, UPSETTER, UPSTROKE

And here are near-alphabets of **RE** and **UN** eight-letter words:

REASCENT	REINDUCT	REQUIGHT
REBODIES	REJACKET	REREWARD
RECANTER	REKINDLE	RESALUTE
REDECIDE	RELUMINE	RETARGET
REEMBODY	REMELTED	REUTTERS
REFRINGE	RENATURE	REVETTED
REGELATE	REOBTAIN	REWIDENS
REHARDEN	REPERUSE	REZONING

UNALLIED	UNJOINTS	UNREINED
UNBEREFT	UNKOSHER	UNSEARED
UNCHASTE	UNLETHAL	UNTAILED
UNDOCILE	UNMODISH	UNUNITED
UNELATED	UNNATIVE	UNVEILER
UNFEUDAL	UNORNATE	UNWINDER
UNGENIAL	UNPOETIC	UNYEANED
UNHAIRED	UNQUIETS	UNZIPPED
UNIDEAED		

Moving on to the suffixes, get your head round a few of these:

ABLE:	ATONABLE, FINDABLE, LAPSABLE, NAMEABLE, SENDABLE
AGE:	BARONAGE, DIALLAGE, INTERAGE, PILOTAGE, STERNAGE

continued

ANT: COSECANT, GALIVANT, PENCHANT, RELEVANT, STAGNANT

ATE: CORELATE, GEMINATE, LEVIRATE, OBTURATE, TITIVATE

ENT: ERUMPENT, FECULENT, PLANGENT, PRURIENT, SCANDENT

IER: BLUESIER, BRICKIER, CRUMMIER, FROGGIER, YOUTHIER

IEST: DULLIEST, LAWNIEST, MOORIEST, RUGGIEST, WHITIEST

ISE/IZE: CAPONISE/IZE, FABULISE/IZE, INFAMISE/IZE, PTYALISE/IZE, SOBERISE/IZE

ISH: CAMELISH, FLIRTISH, POKERISH, SNEAKISH, TILEFISH

IST: CANOEIST, CREOLIST, LUTENIST, PARODIST, TENORIST

LESS: BATHLESS, CODELESS, HOOFLESS, RIFTLESS, WARTLESS

LIKE: CORDLIKE, EPICLIKE, MASTLIKE, SALTLIKE, VESTLIKE

LY: BADGERLY, DATIVELY, GOLDENLY, PLAGUILY, TONISHLY

MAN/MEN: CORPSMAN/MEN, HOTELMAN/MEN, LODESMAN/MEN, POINTMAN/MEN, SHIREMAN/MEN

NESS: AWAYNESS, HERENESS, LONGNESS, NULLNESS, THATNESS

TION: GELATION, LIBATION, NUDATION, PUNITION, SWAPTION

Coming back to those common letters, you need to know a good number of eights with six **RETAINS** letters and two others. Of course, we have seen a lot already – all the **RETAINS + 1** and **RETAINA + 1** words, to start with. However, it can do no harm to look at a few more. But setting out the **ATEBRIN + 1** list, the **CINEAST + 1** list, and so on, would give a long and tedious series of lists, more likely to put readers off than engage their enthusiasm. It also has large numbers of duplicates – **ATEBRIN + C = CERTAIN + B**, and so on. (**BACTERIN**, in case you're wondering).

Likewise, setting them out as '6 + 2' lists could give us some dauntingly long lists – there are 576 combinations of two letters (**AA**, **AB**, and so on, through to **ZZ**) that could go with any six-letter set to form an eight. Obviously, no six letters go with all 576 or even get close, but there comes a time for most people when learning words to improve your game tips over from being interesting to just a chore. Some of you may feel you've passed that stage already.

But just to set out pages of words in no particular order, or even alphabetically, doesn't seem to be any improvement. So take a look at these '6 + 2' lists, which have been limited so as not to try the average reader's patience to exhaustion. Only about thirty two-letter combinations are given for any set of six letters. A maximum of two anagrams are given for any resulting eight-letter combination. And simple **S** endings on sevens we've already met have been excluded, as have eight-letter words we've seen already in other lists.

AEINRS +

AC	CANARIES	CESARIAN	IK	KAISERIN
AG	ANGARIES	ARGINASE	IN	SIRENIAN
BL	RINSABLE		IY	YERSINIA

AEINRS + *continued*

BM	MIRBANES		KM	RAMEKINS	
BU	ANBURIES	URBANISE	KP	RANPIKES	
CK	SKINCARE		LV	RAVELINS	
DL	ISLANDER		LX	RELAXINS	
DY	SYNEDRIA		MU	ANEURISM	
FO	FARINOSE		MY	SEMINARY	
FP	FIREPANS	PANFRIES	NO	RAISONNE	
FS	FAIRNESS	SANSERIF	NW	SWANNIER	
GK	SKEARING		SU	ANURESIS	SENARIUS
GY	RESAYING	SYNERGIA	SX	XERANSIS	
HP	PARISHEN	SERAPHIN	UZ	AZURINES	SUZERAIN

AEINRT +

BC	BACTERIN		LN	INTERNAL	
CC	ACENTRIC		LO	ORIENTAL	RELATION
CU	ANURETIC		LP	TRAPLINE	TRIPLANE
CV	NAVICERT		MN	TRAINMEN	
DH	ANTHERID		MT	MARTINET	
DP	DIPTERAN		MU	RUMINATE	
EH	ATHERINE	HERNIATE	MW	WARIMENT	
EI	INERTIAE		MY	TYRAMINE	
GM	EMIGRANT	REMATING	OP	ATROPINE	
GV	GRIEVANT	VINTAGER	OR	ANTERIOR	
HP	PERIANTH		OT	TENTORIA	
HU	HAURIENT		PU	PAINTURE	
IL	INERTIAL		RW	INTERWAR	

AEINST +

AB	BASANITE		
AC	ESTANCIA		
AF	FANTASIE		
AH	ASTHENIA		
AT	ASTATINE	TANAISTE	
BH	ABSINTHE		
CM	AMNESTIC	SEMANTIC	
CV	CISTVAEN	VESICANT	
DY	DESYATIN		
EV	NAIVETES		
FM	MANIFEST		
GU	SAUTEING	UNITAGES	

GZ	TZIGANES
IP	PIANISTE
KU	UNAKITES
KV	KISTVAEN
MO	SOMNIATE
OV	STOVAINE
OX	SAXONITE
PS	STEAPSIN
PY	EPINASTY
TV	TASTEVIN
UV	SUIVANTE

AEIRST +

AH	HETAIRAS		
AT	ARIETTAS	ARISTATE	
BO	SABOTIER		
CD	ACRIDEST		
CH	STICHERA	THERIACS	
DI	IRISATED		
DK	STRAIKED		
DO	ASTEROID		
DP	DIPTERAS	TARSIPED	
EE	EATERIES		
EP	PARIETES	PETARIES	
EV	EVIRATES		

GT	STRIGATE	
HP	TRIPHASE	
HU	THESAURI	
HY	HYSTERIA	
IM	AIRTIMES	SERIATIM
IX	SEXTARII	
LO	SOTERIAL	
MU	MURIATES	SEMITAUR
MV	VITAMERS	
MW	WARTIMES	
MY	SYMITARE	
PW	WIRETAPS	

AEIRST + *continued*

PY	ASPERITY	VY	VESTIARY
SV	TRAVISES		

AENRST +

AB	ANTBEARS	RATSBANE	EE	SERENATE	
AE	ARSENATE	SERENATA	EF	FENESTRA	
AG	STARAGEN	TANAGERS	EJ	SERJEANT	
AL	ASTERNAL		EO	EARSTONE	RESONATE
AM	SARMENTA	SEMANTRA	EU	SAUTERNE	
AO	ANOESTRA		FO	SEAFRONT	
AV	TAVERNAS	TSAREVNA	GO	RAGSTONE	STONERAG
BD	BANDSTER	BARTENDS	GU	STRAUNGE	
BG	BANGSTER		OR	ANTRORSE	
CD	CANTREDS		OW	STONERAW	
CE	CENTARES	SARCENET	PT	TRANSEPT	TRAPNEST
DO	TORNADES				

AINRST +

AD	INTRADAS	RADIANTS	AZ	TZARINAS	
AG	GRANITAS		BD	ANTBIRDS	
AI	INTARSIA		BG	BRASTING	
AM	MARTIANS	TAMARINS	BO	TABORINS	
AP	ASPIRANT	PARTISAN	CO	CANTORIS	

AINRST + *continued*

DK	STINKARD	
DO	DIATRONS	INTRADOS
DR	TRIDARNS	
DU	UNITARDS	
GK	KARTINGS	STARKING
GW	RINGTAWS	WRASTING
GY	STINGRAY	STRAYING

HO	TRAHISON	
KO	SKIATRON	
LO	TONSILAR	
OP	ATROPINS	
OS	ARSONIST	
OT	STRONTIA	
OU	RAINOUTS	SUTORIAN

EINRST +

CE	ENTERICS	SECRETIN
DD	STRIDDEN	
DO	DRONIEST	
EE	ETERNISE	TEENSIER
EI	ERINITES	NITERIES
EO	ONERIEST	SEROTINE
EX	INTERSEX	
EY	SERENITY	
FI	SNIFTIER	
GH	RIGHTENS	
GL	LINGSTER	TRINGLES
GT	GITTERNS	

GV	STERVING	
IL	NIRLIEST	NITRILES
IO	IRONIEST	
IU	NEURITIS	
KL	LINKSTER	STRINKLE
LU	INSULTER	LUSTRINE
LY	TINSELRY	
OR	INTRORSE	SNORTIER
OY	TYROSINE	
OZ	TRIZONES	
TY	ENTRYIST	
UV	UNRIVETS	VENTURIS

Some purists will be unhappy that we have chosen to give only selections of each of these lists, but this is not a book of word lists only. We have tried to achieve a balance between the lists and the rest of the book, and did not want to overwhelm newcomers to this side of the game with vast unlearnable numbers of new words. For those who want to see full lists from which these are a selection, other books and sources are available, which we'll talk about a little more later.

I have tried to include words which are likely to appear on your rack, and which are also memorable in some way. Perhaps you have been struck by the dependable rhythm of **BEELIKE, FATLIKE, NETLIKE, RATLIKE, TINLIKE**, the unexpected poetry of **GASOLIER, GIRASOLE, SERAGLIO**, or the sheer serendipitousness of discovering that the anagram of **FAIRNESS** is **SANSERIF**. Playing words like **KINGLET, STONERAW**, and **ERUMPENT** will bring a wow factor to your game that everyday words will never match.

So do try and learn as many of these words as you can, even if only a few at a time. Your three-letter words, your clever little parallel plays, and your sticking down **EX** for thirty-six are all very well, but it is the bonuses that will lift your game to a new level. Learn them, use them, treasure them.

Some great puzzles to try

Find as many playable eight-letter words as you can on these boards with the racks shown:

1. Your rack: **A E I N R S T**

2. Your rack: **A E E I N R S**

3. Your rack: **A D E L N T U**

4. Your rack: **A C E I N R T**

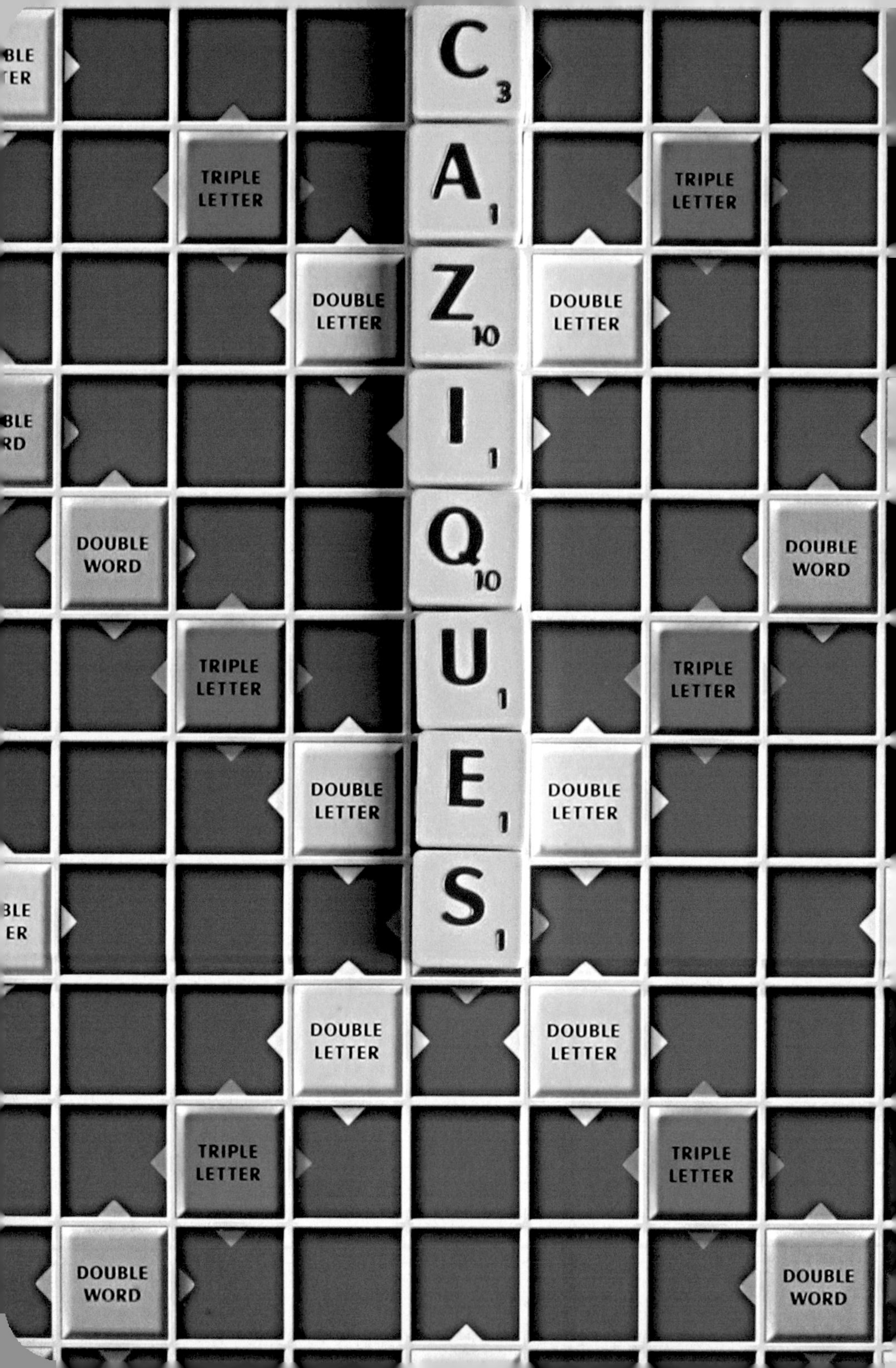
CAZIQUES

9 The end is nigh

So, you've learned your twos, most of your threes, and some useful fours. You've got maximum value from whatever high-value tiles you picked up, and you've used your new-found confidence in finding sevens and eights, especially with an S or a blank, to make a couple of bonus words. The only problem is, your opponent, being one of those annoying people, has done the exact same thing.

Final pointers

You are now approaching the end of the game, and the scores are close. Whether it's about 200 each or 400 each doesn't matter. Your score as such has become irrelevant. You want to win the game.

It won't always happen this way. In a game between two evenly-matched players, one can get all the luck, or just that little bit when it matters, and run out the winner by 200 or 300 points. A weaker player can often beat a stronger one over one game. That's why tournament players always like to settle important tournaments over a number of matches – not necessarily all against the same player, but against a number of players of similar standard. Then the cream tends to rise to the top. A one-off smash-and-grab win proves nothing.

But let's assume you are playing a game now and, with few or no tiles left in the bag, the scores are close. How do you find that vital edge?

Essentially, what you are now trying to do is not just maximize your own score but also minimize your opponent's. And to do that, you need to know what letters your opponent has got, or know as nearly as is possible. You do this by *tile-tracking*.

Back at the beginning of the book we talked about counting up whether more A's or I's had been played, so that, given a choice, you could play whichever there were more of left in the bag, making you less likely to be left with an awkward duplicate. Tile-tracking is an extension of this tactic, and relies on the fact that you know exactly how many of each letter were in the bag at the start of the game. You also know what's been played – it's all there in front of you. And you know what's on your rack. It's simple arithmetic to work out what's left – and that must be what is on your opponent's rack or still in the bag.

I'll repeat again what I said about the A's and I's. A card player – such as in bridge or poker – will always try to remember what cards have been turned over and are therefore not in the hands of the other players or still in the pack to be dealt. It's an accepted – indeed essential – part of good play. So it is in Scrabble, but with the advantage that all that tough memory work is eliminated. Everything that's been played in Scrabble is face up. It's hard enough remembering over 200,000 allowable words without remembering whether or not somebody played the second F twenty minutes ago. Fortunately you don't have to. Just look at the board.

Even better, look at your tile-tracking sheet. A tile-tracking sheet is a pre-prepared list or grid of letters, which you cross off as each tile is played. At the end of the game, what you haven't crossed off is what's still to come.

Different people use different types of tracking sheet. Some list the letters A-Z, plus blank, down one side of the sheet, and make a tick against each as it is played. So towards the end of the game, if there are only eight ticks against the letter A, you know there is one to come, as there are nine in the set.

Some make the relevant number of ticks against each letter at the start of the game and then cross them off, so the number of ticks left is the number of that letter still to be played. Some write out all hundred letters and cross them through as they are played.

Three different styles of tile-tracking sheet, each shown part way through a game:

1.

A	✓✓✓✓✓✓	O	✓✓✓✓✓
B	✓	P	✓✓
C	✓✓	Q	✓
D	✓✓✓	R	✓✓✓✓
E	✓✓✓✓✓✓✓	S	✓✓
F	✓	T	✓✓✓✓✓
G	✓	U	✓✓✓
H	✓✓	V	
I	✓✓✓✓	W	✓✓
J	✓	X	✓
K		Y	✓
L	✓✓✓	Z	✓
M	✓	?	✓
N	✓✓✓✓		

2.

A ✗✗✗✗✓✓✓✓		O ✗✗✗✗✓✓✓✓	
B ✗✓		P ✗✓	
C ✗✓		Q ✗	
D ✗✗✗✓		R ✗✗✗✓✓	
E ✗✗✗✗✗✓✓✓✓✓✓		S ✗✓✓✓	
F ✓✓		T ✗✗✓✓✓✓	
G ✗✗✓		U ✗✗✗✓✓	
H ✗✗		V ✗✓	
I ✗✗✗✗✗✓✓✓		W ✗✗	
J ✓		X ✓	
K ✗		Y ✗✓	
L ✗✗✓✓		Z ✓	
M ✗✗		? ✗✗	
N ✗✗✗✓✓✓			

3.

ÀÀÀÀÀÀÀÀA
ÉÉÉÉÉÉÉÉÉEEE
ÍÍÍÍÍÍÍIII
ØØØØØØOOO
ÚÚÚÚU

J K Ǫ X Ẓ
ɃB ȻȻ ĐØĐD
ƑF ǤǤG ĦĦ
ŁŁLL MM ȠȠȠȠNN
ɎP
ŘŘŘŘRR
ȘȘȘS
ŦŦŦTTT
ɎɎ WW ɎY
ɎɎ

Of course, if you have access to a computer or photo copier, you only need to write or type your tracking sheet out once and then print off a whole batch of them. It is rumoured that some people have been known to use the photocopier in the office for this sort of thing.

Many people still think of tile-tracking as somehow cheating. Coming back to the cards analogy, it has been pointed out that you can't pre-prepare a grid of cards and cross them off as they are played. I certainly wouldn't try it in the local bridge club or poker casino. But in Scrabble, given that you have pen and paper in front of you to keep the score, it would be perverse not to allow it. If I've got seven tiles left on my rack and you've got the last five, there is a far greater level of skill attached to winning the game if each of us knows what the other is holding, rather than both just shooting in the dark.

Note that you shouldn't cross tiles off your tracking sheet when you pick them; you may decide to change, so only eliminate them when they are actually played. If tile-tracking is new to you, you may find you forget to track the occasional move – usually after a bonus – but with the majority crossed off, you can usually rescue the situation with a quick count. If both the B's have been played and you discover you have only crossed off one, chances are that it's one of the moves in which a B was played that you forgot about.

So, you know what your opponent has on his final rack. (To avoid a lot of tiresome uses of 'he or she' and 'his or her', let's say in this instance that the opponent is male). Try to work out what his highest move is, especially if he has a high-scoring tile. If his *next-highest* move is substantially less, play something to block the high-scoring move – unless by doing so you deny yourself a sufficiently high score for your own highest move. Do the arithmetic. If I score sixteen here, he gets thirty-two there. But if I block his thirty-two, even though it only scores me twelve (so I'm 'down four'), he can only get twenty, so he's 'down twelve'. So it must be worth it to block his thirty-two point move.

The other main consideration in endgame play is playing out (i.e. getting rid of all your tiles to finish the game) as quickly as possible. When you're down to your final tiles, try to play a move which will allow you to play *all your remaining tiles* in the next move. That means you need two places to play out, so that even if your opponent blocks one, you still have the other. Conversely, you must look to see if your opponent only has one place to play out – and if so, block it.

It's surprising how often it's worth accepting a score that might be lower than your optimal score by quite a few points, if it enables you to play out at your next move. You deny your opponent another score, and get the value of his remaining tiles added to your score, and he gets the same value deducted. That usually adds up to a sizable swing that can make all the difference in a tight game.

Have a look at this board from my good friend and Scrabble genius Phil Appleby:

Your rack: **I I N O S S T**

You are thirteen points behind, and, having tile-tracked, you know your opponent has **D E K O R**. What points do you need to consider for your next move? What would you play? Take a few minutes to examine the board and decide what you would do.

Your opponent has one place to play out – by playing **FORKED** using the floating **F** near the bottom left-hand corner. You must block this play, and play something that will enable you to play out in the following move. Look for his next-best score, and work out whether you can score enough to win the game. If not, look again.

Assuming your opponent has a good knowledge of three- and four-letter words, he can play **KEB** or **KOB** on the top left triple word square, for twenty-seven. **DREK** or **DEEK**, using the E of **OYEZ** and also making **KO**, notches up twenty-five. His best score is **ROED**, played directly under the **AINE** of **MORAINE**, also making **AR**, **IO**, **NE**, and **JOBED**, which scores thirty-three.

Endgame problems can get very complex, and computer power (not available during a real game, obviously) has to be harnessed to be sure of getting the optimal path for each player. But, without bringing in the Pentagon supercomputer, one good play for you would be **MOIST**, using the **M** of **MORAINE** and making four two-letter words. That scores you twenty-seven, and blocks your opponent's **FORKED**. If he now plays his next-best **ROED**, you go down to the bottom-right triple word square and play out with **SIN/WARDENS/GI**, which would give you a fourteen-point win. If your opponent, rather than playing **ROED**, blocks your **SIN** outplay, such as by playing **GO/OD**, he gets a much smaller score and you can win by playing **SIN** elsewhere, such as making **SIN/JOBES**.

The two important things here are that you blocked his **FORKED**, and you left yourself more than one place to play out your remaining letters. And unlike other Scrabble situations, where the best move is all about the balance of probabilities, maximizing your chances, seeing what way the wind's blowing, and hoping for the best, working out a winning endgame can, if you can find the right path, give you a guaranteed win without trusting to luck. It's an immensely satisfying feeling to get it right and know you've won a game you could, with a little less care, have lost.

Endgames need a lot of practice; they also, as you can see in the example above, need a good knowledge of the shorter words. And one further difficulty – it's much harder working out what your opponent might do, even if you know what tiles he is holding, when you can't physically see those tiles in front of you. In a recent game, I worked out that my opponent's final tiles were **DEEEMRT**, and duly blocked what I thought was her best score (probably something like **ME** for twenty) while making sure I could play out next move. What I completely missed was that she had the word **METERED**, which she duly played with great glee for seventy-odd points to win the game. I wouldn't have missed **METERED** if I'd had those tiles in front of me on my own rack (or at least I hope I wouldn't), but it's that much harder when you're looking at the letters scribbled in a corner of a crowded piece of paper.

There are other elements to endgame strategy. For example, if you have a high-scoring tile which you can't score much with on the board as it stands, you might be able to set yourself up an unblockable high score with it next time.

Your rack: **A A C D E I X**

Opponent's rack: **C N R U Y**

Without showing the whole board, let's assume there is nowhere for you to score much with your **X**. If you play **ACID** in the second-top row, also making **AA** and **CH**, you can then play out in the next move with **AXE** along the top row, also making **ACH/XI/ED** and scoring sixty-six points. If your opponent uses the **D** to make **DUN** or **DRY**, you still get sixty for **AX** – not an outplay, but probably enough to win even a semi-close game. It will rarely, if ever, work out quite as neatly as that, but always see if you can use your perfect knowledge of your opponent's rack to set yourself up a move like this if you have a high-scoring tile on your rack at the endgame.

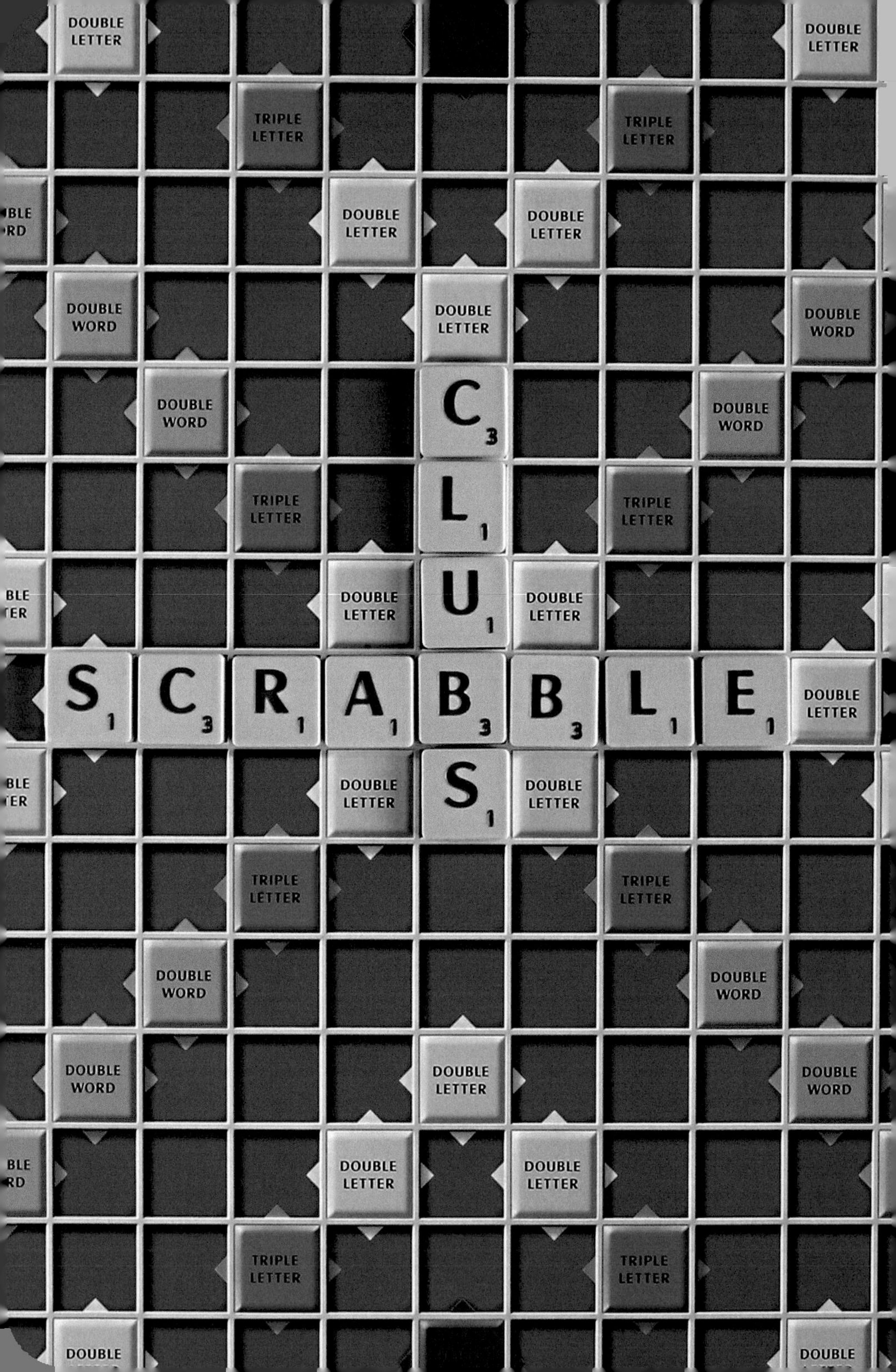
CLUES
SCRABBLE

10 Clubs and tournaments

So, you've had your appetite whetted for trying to move your Scrabble game up a level or two. You want to squeeze more points out of every move with neat little parallel plays using two- and three-letter words, you want to play some impressive bonuses, and then eke out a win with a well-thought-out endgame.

Clubs and tournaments

The only problem is, if your Scrabble-playing friends/relatives/ dog (clever boy though he is) don't want to come on this journey with you, you are pitched into an endless round of 'What does that mean?' and 'That's not a proper word'.

Even showing Auntie Mary that **XU**, **JIZ**, or **ETESIAN** is there in black and white in *Collins Scrabble Dictionary* is unlikely to appease her. Learning useful words and good techniques to improve your game is seen as unsportsmanlike, almost cheating. So your next move has to be to take a deep breath and move into the wonderful world of your local Scrabble club.

People have some odd ideas about Scrabble clubs – that's if they realize they exist at all. They are assumed to be patronized solely by either elderly ladies in pink cardigans clutching flasks of tea and inedible home-made biscuits, or geeky guys taking an evening off from working out the square root of minus one. While I can't quite guarantee you won't meet anyone at all like that, most Scrabble club members are normal, well-adjusted people who want nothing more than a sociable evening out and a good game of Scrabble. And the tea-toting ladies and odd guys are usually pretty nice once you get to know them.

You can find the whereabouts of your local Scrabble club by writing to the:
Scrabble Clubs Manager
J W Spear and Sons PLC
Mattel House
Vanwall Road
Maidenhead, SL6 4UB.

Or if you're of a more technological turn of mind, try chucking 'Scrabble' and your home town into your internet search engine and see what comes up.

So what happens at a Scrabble club? It's impossible to be definitive, as each will be run in a slightly different way. Some will have a very informal approach, where you just turn up and play anyone else sitting around waiting for a game. Others are more structured, where you all start at the same time and the organizer tells you who to play. Others again have a league table where you have to play everyone, or everyone in your division, once or twice in a season (however long a season may be), but within that you arrange your own games at times to suit.

However, a few things are pretty much universal at any Scrabble club in the country (and, I imagine, the world). There will presumably be a meeting place and a regular evening when the club meets (although the large and venerable London Scrabble League, of which I have the honour to be chairman, arranges four-player fixtures in members' homes). There will either be tables about the size of card tables for individual games, or longer trestle tables that can accommodate a few games at a time. Players generally supply their own Scrabble sets and other paraphernalia, so take yours if possible. Crucially, tea and coffee will be supplied either as part of your entry fee or subscription, or for a small charge.

Here are a few other ways in which playing at a club may be different from how you are used to playing at home:

De luxe sets

Most clubs insist on, or at least give preference to, de luxe sets; these have boards which are on a turntable so that they can be moved to face each player, and tiles that click into the square on which they are played so that they don't move around when the board is turned, accidentally nudged, or otherwise moved. Nothing detracts more from the pleasure of the game than continually having to realign the tiles so that you can read the words properly, or having to twist your neck to try to read the board upside-down. You don't read a book or newspaper upside-down, so why try to do it with a Scrabble board? If Christmas or your birthday is coming up, you might try having a word with the appropriate person and, with a bit of luck, you'll have a big, square parcel to open on The Day.

Smooth tiles

As you now know, the most valuable tiles in the bag are the blanks. For that reason, it is slightly unsatisfactory that you can sometimes, accidentally or deliberately, feel that a tile in the bag is a blank. Smooth tiles prevent any suspicion that a player has been feeling in the bag for a blank tile.

This is not to suggest that cheating by feeling for the blank is common. I have played a lot of Scrabble, sometimes with a fair amount of money, pride, or self-esteem at stake, and cheating of any kind is extremely rare. If my opponent pulls both blanks from the bag, or the second blank when there are only three or four tiles left, I don't immediately suspect that he is fingering the tiles before he selects. But if I get both blanks, or one vital one, I feel happier if we're playing with smooth tiles. Indeed, if the bag contains two tiles of which one is a blank, and you have to pick one, it can be difficult **not** to feel whether you've got it, be your intentions as pure as a busload of nuns at a Cliff Richard concert.

The newest sets do contain smooth tiles. However, the box design has not changed from the previous edition, which shops will presumably continue to sell off for some time. So there is no way you can actually tell whether you are getting smooth tiles or not when you buy a new set. So, as with everything else in Scrabble, there is a certain element of luck involved.

Playing one opponent at a time

Quite simply, Scrabble is a game for two players. The rules that come with your set may say you can play with up to four, but the two-person game is far superior. You cannot form a strategy, nor can you plan ahead in any way, if there are two or even three more people to play between your last turn and your next one. Apart from that, it's just boring playing with three or four players – you are only involved in the game a third or a quarter of the time, and if one or two of your opponents are slow, you can have an interminable wait till it comes round to you again. Sure, you can be looking for what you might play when it eventually becomes your turn, but only to a limited extent. You have no way of knowing if your opponents' plays will drive a coach and horses through the place you were going to make your move – or if they might give you a better one.

In club and tournament play, if the numbers are odd, one person will sit out for a round, rather than subjecting three people to the triangle of doom. Alternatively, one player may take on two players at once, but in two completely separate games on two separate boards. This is an excellent way of sharpening up your Scrabble reflexes, rather like a chess simul, a form of chess match where one (usually superior) player takes on a number of others simultaneously.

Use of *Collins Scrabble Words* for all adjudications

It's very annoying when you play a word, only to have it disallowed – especially if, the week before, you were allowed to play it. It's even more maddening if your opponent the week before was allowed to play it. Use *Collins Scrabble Words* to adjudicate on any challenges. This lists every allowable word in strict alphabetical order except that very long words, those with ten letters or more, are confined to a separate section at the end. No arguing about the plural of *octopus* or whether you can have *sublimer* or *honestest*.

By using the most recent edition of *Collins Scrabble Words* the allowable word list is kept up to date; new words are being coined or accepted into English all the time, and you don't want to be prevented from playing **EMAIL, EURO, CHAV, ZIT, BIRYANI,** or any of a host of others.

Using a large word source is the only way to bring into play the wealth of fascinating words which we have been looking at throughout this book, and which your own dictionary may not have. Some people feel that the more words are allowed in the game, the more it becomes just a memory exercise. Learning the words is certainly important, but having a large number of words at his disposal allows a player to display a fuller range of Scrabble skills than would otherwise be the case.

Whether this theory is infinitely expandable is open to debate. Using the full twenty-volume OED may be a few steps too far. But suffice to say that every dictionary is different; there is no such thing as a definitive 'list of English words', and *Collins Scrabble Words* has more than most.

If you haven't, or haven't yet, got *Collins Scrabble Words*, you and your fellow-players will have to do a bit of adjudicating from time to time. A dictionary will generally list only a base word, such as **TABLE**. It will not specifically show **TABLES, TABLED, TABLING,** or **TABLINGS**. Before starting play it's worth agreeing a few guidelines as to what you're going to allow and what you aren't.

For instance, nouns, fairly obviously, have a plural. But all nouns? If you watch *Countdown* you will have become familiar with the concept of **count nouns** and **mass nouns**. A count noun is something you can have more than one of, and therefore the noun takes a plural. **MAN, HORSE,** and **BANANA** are all count nouns with obvious plurals. It needn't be a thing you can touch – **DAY, LIE,** and **FEELING** are also count nouns.

The problems start, if you allow them to, with the mass noun. Can you pluralize words like **TENNIS**, **CALCITE**, and **FLU**? *Countdown* will often say no, declaring that they are mass nouns, so you can't have more than one of them. My advice about this is – forget it. Any noun can have a plural. Go ahead and allow **TENNISES**, **CALCITES**, and **FLUS**. *Collins Scrabble Words* certainly does.

What is not always so easy to work out is what the plural actually is. We know that it is usually formed by adding **-s**. There are some well-known exceptions – so well-known, in fact, that you barely register them. Nouns ending in **-s**, **-ch**, or **-sh** all add **-es** – **TENNISES**, **CHURCHES**, **BRUSHES**. (As usual, there are exceptions to the exceptions – words ending in the Scottish *ch*, like **LOCH**, just add **-s** in the plural).

Words ending in **-y** preceded by a consonant change the **-y** to **-ies** – **FLIES**, **BERRIES**. And of course we have **MEN**, **MICE**, **SHEEP** and plenty of other common irregular plurals.

But what is the plural of **TROUT**? Usually it would just be **TROUT**, as in 'I caught six trout.' But could it ever be valid to say **TROUTS**? Remember **TROUT** has an informal meaning of a silly or unpleasant person. 'The neighbours round here are a right bunch of trout'. That sounds odd. 'A right bunch of trouts', surely. And sometimes you need a bit more technical knowledge. Is **RADIUSES** an acceptable alternative to **RADII** as the plural of **RADIUS**? It's at moments like these that you do need to go to the dictionary – preferably always the same one. For the record, *Collins Scrabble Words* allows **TROUTS** and **RADIUSES**.

What about verbs? Again, it's fairly simple on the face of it. We have the **-s**, **-ed**, and **-ing** endings; thus **CONTAIN** leads to **CONTAINS**, **CONTAINED**, and **CONTAINING**. If the verb ends in **-e**, drop the **e** before adding **-ed** or **-ing**, as in **STROKED**, **STROKING**. And we have a similar **-y** adjustment to the one we have with nouns, as in **MARRIES**, **MARRIED**. Then there is the doubling, in certain circumstances, of a final consonant before **–ED** and **–ING**, as in **STRUMMED**, **STRUMMING**. Hmm, that's quite a few exceptions already, all of which we handle in normal speech and writing without a moment's thought. But if we think of short, simple verbs, there seem to be more exceptions than adherents to the rule – **RUN**, **SWIM**, **BUILD**, **TAKE**, **GO**, **DO**, **SPEAK**, **PAY**, **EAT**, **DRINK**, and **MAKE** all deviate from the **-ed** form. Again, there is no substitute for a good dictionary if you want to be sure of the irregularities.

Now for the adjectives. Ah, adjectives! Before the advent of *Collins Scrabble Words*, no element of word adjudication caused more problems than whether you could add **-er** and **-est** to an adjective. **POLITER, STERILEST, WHOLER, HONESTEST, UNFITTER, LIVEST, DEADEST** – these and many like them caused hours of harmless merriment, and the occasional tantrum, as their acceptability or otherwise was debated.

The second-best solution is to start your own list. If you allow, say, **NUBILER**, put it on an 'allowed' list and keep it with your set or tuck it into your dictionary. Similarly, if you decide that **EDIBLER** is a comparative too far, it goes on your 'disallowed list'. Then, when the word comes up next week or next year, you can at least be consistent. But you still have the problem of deciding which list it goes on in the first place – and when one of you has played the word and there are only the two of you there, a one-each stalemate on whether the word should be valid is almost inevitable. The best solution – buy *Collins Scrabble Words*. If it's in there, the word is valid; if it ain't, it ain't.

Playing to win

As I've emphasized throughout this book, it's not what you score that counts, it's whether you score more than your opponent. It's a statement of the obvious, surely. Don't we always play a game to win?

In the early days of the National Scrabble Championship (NSC), the winner was the person with the highest total score over a set number of games. It didn't matter whether you actually won the games or not. So if you could score 500 or so in all your games, even if you lost one or two, this was better than plodding along scoring 300-400 but making sure you always won. This led to a highly artificial form of the game where your opponent effectively became your partner.

Why? Consider it this way. In a big tournament like the NSC, with 100 or more players, you just knew that one of them was going to get lucky and average over 500 per game. So you had to give yourself a chance of being that lucky player. Thus you played a very open game, which means you tried to make lots of places on the board where bonus words would fit in. In particular, you tried to place a letter between two triple word squares, opening the row or column for the chance of playing a nine-timer – a bonus word starting on one triple word square and finishing on the next. This meant your score was multiplied by nine and received the extra fifty to boot. This guaranteed a score of over 100 for a move – sometimes much more if you used some high-scoring tiles.

a board with one tile in a triple word row or column

the same board with a 9-timer played in the position

Any player who didn't get at least one of these 'nine-timers' per game knew they couldn't win the tournament. So you had to have a tacit agreement with your partner-opponent not to close these spaces off for a small score. They had to be left for the nine-timer. And if your opponent got there first, well, you'd had your chance and you just had to create another opening elsewhere on the board.

Eventually most players realized this was a silly way to play, and what was called matchplay Scrabble took over. Quite simply this meant, playing to win: scoring 500 is pointless if your opponent gets 501. Striving to open places for high-scoring bonuses; heroically resisting the temptation to block them for only a moderately high score; keeping them for the very high one instead: all these strategies were swept away. You played whatever way you liked. Keep the board open, keep it blocked, tie it in knots if you want to. Just win the game. At the end of the tournament, the player who had won the most games was the winner.

Having said that, you can't afford to neglect the possibility of high scores, because players on the same number of wins are ranked according to their 'spread'. This is the total points scored by you minus the total points scored by all your opponents – the equivalent of goal difference in football. So, at least at the beginning of a tournament or club competition, and at the end if you're in contention, it's nice to stick in a really high score, as long as your opponent doesn't score almost as much (or even more).

When matchplay Scrabble became widespread in the Eighties, a different and somewhat bizarre method was used to separate players on the same number of wins. This was called **Sum of Opponents' Scores** (SOS) and the gist of it was that those on equal wins were ranked according to the total number of wins achieved by all their opponents at that tournament. The idea was that if you had a higher SOS, you had played stronger opponents and therefore deserved to be placed higher in the table.

One result of this was that winning or losing the game was literally all that mattered. Scores, spreads, and everything else were irrelevant. If, before a game was completed, you decided that you could not possibly win, you could just resign, allowing you to hit the bar or at least the tea trolley early to drown your sorrows.

However, it was realized fairly early on that SOS didn't really prove anything, and it was quickly superseded by spread. But note that spread is a very different thing from score. Spread takes into account not just your score but also what your opponent scores against you, so you must always be alert to denying chances to your opponent as well as getting a good score yourself.

So what all that boils down to for you is this. Don't just think of your move as a score of ten, twenty, thirty, whatever. See how it affects the board before you play it. Check if it opens up any high-scoring opportunities, which your opponent is almost bound to take. If it does, try to find an alternative, less risky move elsewhere.

The playing of **CARE** would be a risky move here, as you have opened a triple-word chance for your opponent if he has an **S**, **D**, **R**, **T**, or even **X** for **CAREX**.

Sometimes, after a tournament, a non-playing friend might ask me, 'What kind of scores did you get?' The truth is, I can rarely remember. But I do remember that I won one out of six, twelve out of twelve, eight out of seventeen, or whatever.

Both players keep the score

If you are playing to win, it follows that you need to know whether you are winning or losing, and by how much, at any particular time. If you're behind, you may need to take a bit of a risk and make some openings. If you're ahead, you should be trying to close things up. So make sure you keep the score. If your opponent is of a like mind – fine, both keep score. In any case, it's useful to have a check – mistakes are easily made.

When you try all these these things for yourself

good to know

There are about 330 Scrabble clubs in Britain, and a further 200 or so in schools.

at a club, as well as involving yourself in the higher standard of play, you will be rewarded by finding Scrabble suddenly just feels like a better game.

There are a few other ways in which club play and home play differ. The moment when your shot is over is defined carefully. If timers are being used, it's the moment you press the button to stop your own timer and start your opponent's; without timers, it's the moment you announce your score. Until that point of no return is passed, you can take your tiles back and change your mind.

From this, it follows that you shouldn't challenge your opponent's move until he has pressed that timer or announced that score; by doing so, you alert him to the fact that you think the word is wrong, and he may take the opportunity to think again.

Lifting the tile-bag

Another thing newcomers to a club find quite odd is the sight of players lifting the bag well clear of the table when they pick new tiles. The rule is that the bag should be lifted to shoulder height, thus precluding any possibility of cheating by having a sly look in the bag as it lies on the table or as you hold it under your nose. As with the 'feelable blanks', this is not to say that cheating was rife before this rule was introduced; merely that it is better to eliminate the possibility of cheating rather than having any unwarranted suspicions lingering around the name of an honest player.

No late changes

Apart from a few details introduced mainly to
facilitate the use of timers, the actual rules of the
game at a club are exactly the same as you are
used to at home – with one exception: you can't
change when there are fewer than seven tiles left
in the bag.

This rule was introduced back in the dark days
when a **Q** picked late in the game was likely to be
unplayable. It prevented a player throwing a **Q** back
into the bag at the last moment, in an attempt to
foist it on his opponent. Nowadays, with **QI**, **QAT**,
and so on at our disposal, a last-minute **Q** is not
such a nightmare, but the rule persists. It may be
fair to say that you shouldn't be allowed to put a **Q**,
a **J**, a **V**, or some other unplayable junk back in the
bag at the very end, forcing your opponent to pick
it if he wants to make a move. On the other hand, a
more hard-nosed player may think it should all be
part of the game. But at the moment, once there
are six tiles in the bag or fewer, whatever you've
got on your rack is what you're stuck with.

Tournament play

This has the same rules as club play, but it's a
difference of atmosphere more than anything else.
Everyone is trying that bit harder and their play is
that bit sharper.

Tournaments are generally divided into divisions,
so that you play people roughly of your own
standard. Also, tournaments are usually played
under the Swiss system, which means that, as far
as possible, you play someone on the same
number of wins as yourself. However they are

arranged, everyone plays in every round, so there is no danger of travelling half the length of the country and only playing one game because you lose in the first round.

A one-day tournament will normally be held over six rounds. Weekend tournaments over two days can have between eleven and sixteen rounds. Sometimes, usually on a holiday weekend, they are played over three days, with between seventeen and nineteen rounds. Occasionally there are even weeklong tournaments. If you fancy having a go at a tournament, get in touch with the Association of British Scrabble Players. The ABSP regulates tournament play in the UK, and you'll find a very useful calendar of events on their website, **www.absp.org.uk**

Perhaps I can best give you the flavour of a tournament by taking you through a typical two-dayer:

Saturday lunchtime: Arrive at hotel and check into your room. Find brochure extolling the local sights and attractions. Ignore it completely. You can sightsee any time – there's Scrabble to be played.

Buy lunch (if you haven't taken the thrifty option of bringing it with you).

1.30 pm: Players (anything between fifty and a couple of hundred) gather in the playing area. Greet old friends and avoid old enemies. A tense, expectant buzz starts to arise as the 2 pm kick-off approaches.

2.15: People start to look at their watches and wonder why they aren't playing yet. Eventually it is revealed that either (a) someone is late and everyone else is being held up to wait for him, (b) someone is complaining they've been put in the wrong division, or (c) the computer isn't working.

2.30: At last, you hear the familiar rasp of a computer printer, printing out the first round's fixtures. The list is stuck on the wall, with a resulting rugby scrum as everyone tries to see their opening fate. Smaller players often have to wait several minutes until the crowd clears.

The computer will have decreed your opponent, whether you have the opening move, and which table you play at. As there is a slight advantage in having the first move, these are equalized as far as possible over the course of a tournament.

2.40: With everyone finally sitting at the right table, chatting to their opponent, and nervously shuffling tile-bags, the Tournament Director will make a few opening remarks, usually centred around the need for everyone to keep quiet while play is in progress. Nobody can hear him because of the noise.

2.45: At last, it's eyes down and an unnatural silence descends as play starts. At this point, almost invariably, one pair realize they don't have a timer or sometimes even a board, resulting in some local disturbance until everyone is fully equipped and playing.

When a player wants to challenge a word, it is

good to know

The use of timers, the rating system, and the Swiss system of arranging fixtures are all based on similar procedures used in chess tournaments. So was the 'Sum of Opponents' Scores' procedure mentioned earlier in this chapter.

written on one of the pre-printed sheets which have been supplied to every table. The sheet is held up and a runner takes it to the adjudicator's table, where it is marked as allowed or disallowed, and then returned to its home table. The decision brings anything from mild disappointment to anguished despair from one party, and a silent gloat from the other.

The runners, who are often the young children of some of the players, probably have the hardest job at a Scrabble tournament. Their task is footsore, tedious, and thankless. They are liable to be harangued by players for not bringing the challenge-sheet back quickly enough, which is a bit rough on an eight-year-old at any time but especially when, as sometimes happens, the haranguer is their own mother, all maternal instinct subjugated by the fever of competition.

3.15: Noise levels start to rise as the first games finish, and players begin the post-mortems, explaining exactly why they won (superior skill) or lost (sheer bad luck). The Director appeals for quiet. Quiet descends for about five seconds, then wells up again in an uncontrollable crescendo, which means players in the slower games have to finish off to a cacophany of background noise – a Tower of Scrabble.

3.45: With all results in, the computer chunters out the second round fixtures and the whole operation starts again.

4.30: A welcome tea-break, for which the hotel catering staff sometimes even remember to bring the tea.

6.30: Dinner-time. Some players go to their rooms to freshen up, some hit the bar, while some – you've guessed it – fit in a quick friendly game of Scrabble.

8.30: Having eaten twice as much as usual, players file back to the playing room for two more rounds, their digestive systems complaining mightily and in some cases audibly.

10.30: Bleary-eyed, they stagger from the playing room, one or two exultant with six wins out of six, a couple despondent at six losses, but most somewhere in the middle. A few go for an early night, but even the most abstemious tend to discover the need for some alcohol at this point. And yes, even now there are some friendlies starting up in dark corners of the bar, to the astonishment of the hotel's other clientele.

Sunday morning: With play restarting at the unearthly hour of 9.30, it's an unaccustomed early breakfast for most, with a few pale faces and shaky demeanours indicating some over-indulgence the night before, now of course regretted. Notes are compared on how much sleep everybody didn't get, and the usual hotel-type complaints are rife: 'My room was right above the disco.' 'I couldn't turn the heating on.' 'I couldn't turn the heating off.' 'I missed my kids/dog/cat/goldfish.' (Rarely husband or wife, I find.)

9.30: Generally everyone manages to show up on time, if not always in the best of condition. The standard of play does not tend to be of the highest at this part of the weekend.

11.30: By the end of the mid-morning coffee break, players are approaching a state akin to humanity, but for most, it's too late. Only a few are still in with a chance of carrying off the prizes; the rest are playing only for pride and ratings points.

Ratings points are a system whereby everyone who has played in a tournament is accorded a **tournament rating**. This is a figure arrived at by an arithmetical calculation based on the ratings of your opponents, and how many games you win and lose. So the more you win and the stronger your opponents are, the higher your rating. Your most recent tournament ratings are averaged out on a rolling weighted average basis to calculate your actual rating. And if you haven't a clue what a rolling weighted average is, join the club.

Working out your rating for one tournament is not too difficult, but working out your actual rating, which takes into account several tournaments (once you've played several tournaments, obviously) is a major mathematical task. It used to be more or less possible to do on the back of an envelope, but since the introduction of the rolling weighted average, which is designed to give more weight to your most recent games, the calculation requires sums like 1,542,823 divided by 10,050. Basically, you have to trust the Ratings Officer to get it right.

Difficulties of calculation notwithstanding, the ratings give everyone a figure by which they can measure how well they are doing. If your rating is eighty you can aim for ninety, if it's 130 you can go for 140, and if it's 180 you can try to squeeze it up to 185. The top-rated UK players have a rating of around 200, while those at the bottom of the list are rated about sixty. It should be noted that the person at the bottom, even though he or she is, say, 600th out of 600 on the list of rated players, is still the 600th-best of the several million people who play Scrabble. Or at least, he or she can claim to be until some of the others put themselves on the line by entering a tournament, which that person has at least had the nerve to do.

Sunday lunch: There is usually only one game to play after Sunday lunch, so by now everyone is getting a bit stir crazy. Of those still in contention, the divisional winners and the ultimate tournament winner will probably be those who hold their nerve, and who have kept some mental energy in reserve for the final battle. Or, of course, it might just be the ones who get lucky and pick good tiles.

And finally: Amidst rising tension and many pleas for quiet, which are often louder than the noise that gives rise to them, the final round is played and the destinations of the trophies and the prize-money are decided. After one last tea-break, while sweating organizers collate the final results, the winners are announced and applauded, goodbyes are said till next time, and then everybody emerges into the unaccustomed daylight to reacquaint themselves with the outside world.

Tournaments are such intense affairs (if you let them become so) that it is easy to forget to leave the hotel, for the entire day-and-a-bit between checking in and going home, even just for five minutes of fresh air.

Sunday evening: Arrive home, on either a high or a low depending on whether your results have been triumphant or disappointing. With a headache from too much Scrabble, too much eating and drinking, and too long sitting in a traffic jam on the M1, you immediately check to see when the next tournament is.

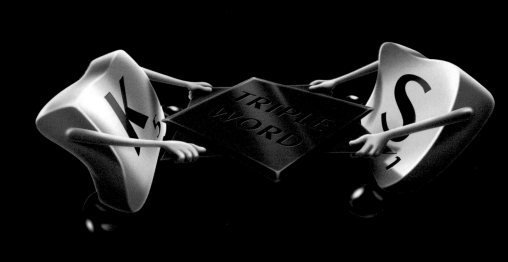

11 Reaching for the top

One of the best aspects of getting involved in the Scrabble club and tournament scene is that, even if you don't immediately feel ready to take on the very best players, you can still mix with them, get to know them, and learn from them. With most competitions being divided into divisions, you can rub shoulders with the top boys and girls without the risk to your ego of actually having to play them.

Playing with the best

Go along to some tournaments, especially the bigger ones and you will find that restaurant, bar, and tea-room are a mix of potential world champions, the greenest of newcomers, and everything in between.

Not many other pastimes can say this. If you take up golf, you'll have to advance pretty high up the ladder even to get into the same room as Tiger Woods, never mind the same tee (unless you pay some vast sum of money for the privilege).

I'm not implying that leading players are worthy of some sort of hero-worship just because they happen to be good at Scrabble. But it's nice to think that when you see so-and-so has become National or perhaps even World Champion, you can say, 'Ah, he's the chap who told me the anagram of **BOOSTING*** during a coffee-break last year in Nottingham'.

Once you've taken that first step of venturing along to a local club, the whole vista of how to get more out of Scrabble starts to open out for you. You will find out where to get hold of the better equipment that adds so much to the game but may not be available in your local shops. Many players now have personalized boards made to their own design (so much classier than a personalized number plate). Round boards, which can be turned without knocking over racks, cups of tea, etc, are particularly popular.

* **BONGOIST**

Someone will tell you about computer programs, electronic pocket gizmos of various kinds, or even good old-fashioned books, any or all of which you can use to improve your word power and check where you might have done better in an actual game. And sooner or later you will be pointed in the direction of a pile of application forms, and before you know it you will be informing your family that someone else is going to have to cook the dinner four weeks on Sunday because you're going to be two hundred miles away playing Scrabble.

Charting your progress comes more or less automatically as you start to play. Most clubs will have a league table, in some format or other, that you will be trying to work your way up. And of course, once you get that first tournament rating, improving it will become, even if you don't quite like to admit it, something of an obsession. If all goes well, you will find that you are soon out of the bottom division, and Division C, Division B, then the hallowed surrounds of Division A will beckon.

If you really get your Scrabble skills and word power motoring, there are even more rarefied heights for which you can aim. There is an annual Masters Tournament for the leading sixteen players in the country. And the pinnacle of the game, held every two years, is the World Championship. This one is very much by invitation only – you have to be one of the top ten or so British players to take part. Although it's an individual tournament, not a team event, it's still a thrill to feel you are representing your country, perhaps in some far-flung corner of the world. You have the pleasure of meeting Scrabble players from many other countries. Play is in English so there are players from Britain and Ireland, America, Canada, Australia, New Zealand, and several African and Asian countries where English is either the first or a popular second language.

World Championships do at times give rise to some interesting culture clashes and vocabulary blank spots. One player from a country where they are used to more exotic vegetables challenged **CELERIES** (you remember that any noun can have a plural), while a former champion from America challenged a British player's move of **LORRY**.

But I wouldn't suggest you worry about such distant targets just yet. Concentrate on getting a good grip of some of the basics in this book, such as the twos, the threes, making good use of JQXZ, trying for bonuses by balancing your rack between vowels and consonants, keeping those bonus-friendly tiles (especially blank and S), and learning some of the sevens and eights that they make. Then either get your regular opponents to do the same, or join a Scrabble club. May the little elf who lives in the bag and puts the tiles into your hand take a liking to you, and I wish you many hours of happy and stimulating Scrabble playing.

World Scrabble Champions:

1991	London	Peter Morris (Canada)
1993	New York	Mark Nyman (UK)
1995	London	David Boys (Canada)
1997	Washington DC	Joel Sherman (USA)
1999	Melbourne	Joel Wapnick (Canada)
2001	Las Vegas	Brian Cappelletto (Canada)
2003	Kuala Lumpur	Panupol Sujjayakorn (Thailand)
2005	London	Adam Logan (Canada)

12 Other forms of Scrabble

Over the years, some players have taken to experimenting with other ways of playing Scrabble, apart from sitting facing your opponent across a table and playing to the standard rules of the game. Various ideas have come and gone. Some take hold and become popular alternatives, others vanish almost as soon as they appear, like an April snowfall, or a pop star's marriage.

Not just a green board

Many people will have had their first introduction to the game in the form of **Junior Scrabble** or some other children's version of the game. Junior Scrabble has a board with preprinted words in a Scrabble game format, and players have to pick tiles which match the letters on the board and play them in the appropriate squares.

The back of the board has yet another version of the game, somewhat more challenging than Junior Scrabble but not quite up to the complexity of the real thing. Mattel currently produce a range of Scrabble games for younger players, including Simpsons Scrabble, which involves among other things Bart stealing Triple Word Squares from an ever more exasperated Homer. This author has not had the pleasure of playing Simpsons Scrabble yet, but it sounds immense fun.

At the other end of the scale, rumours abound of an adult version of the game which is said to be popular with the student population. The details must however remain beyond the scope of a family-oriented volume such as this.

No game would be complete today without its computer version. There are various forms of **Computer Scrabble** for sale, most of which have features such as allowing you to play the computer at different levels, thus putting your opponent at a standard of anything from beginner to expert. You can set the computer to tell you what it would have played with your letters, and, being a computer, it has the annoying property, when set at the top level, of never missing a seven-letter word or other good play, thus gradually shredding your confidence as it points out all the bonuses you missed. Happily you can always switch it off, an option I would dearly love to have with certain human opponents I can think of.

Another way of playing the game is **Duplicate Scrabble**. This is a method used for large tournaments, and involves every player sitting at their own table with their own set. You do not have an opponent – or rather, everyone else in the room is your opponent. A Master of Ceremonies will draw seven tiles, and each player then has a set time to come up with the highest-scoring move they can make with those tiles. Each player scores according to his or her move, but then the highest-scoring move is announced, and every player who did not play that move removes their own play from their board, and substitutes the highest-scoring move.

Play continues by the MC drawing as many tiles as are necessary to replenish the rack to seven in the normal way, and each player, using the tiles which are already on the board and their new rack of seven tiles, again has to find the highest-scoring move they can. This process goes on until all the tiles have been used or no further plays are possible, with the player achieving the highest total for the game obviously being the winner.

The advantage of Duplicate is that the luck element is eliminated; every player has the exact same rack and the exact same board at every move, thus in theory the best player should always win. While this is a big advantage, there are a number of downsides to Duplicate. The skills of rack management, accepting a lower score this time in the hope of a much higher one next time, do not apply. You are simply looking for the highest score you can every time; if you can get one extra point for adding an **S**, you do so. There is no question of playing in certain positions to try to open up the board, close it off, or anything else. Only the score for that move is important.

Duplicate Scrabble also loses an important social aspect of the game. There is less to talk about afterwards. The 'If-only-I'd-played-this-you-wouldn't-have-been-able-to-play-that' type of conversation so beloved of Scrabble players doesn't take place. No clever play such as holding back a **U** because there are only half a dozen tiles left in the bag and the **Q** is not played yet. If you need that **U** to obtain the highest possible score now, you have to play it.

It's all a bit like grabbing what you can at a buffet while the going's good, as against sitting down to a civilized meal where you take your time and leave some room for dessert.

Duplicate is the form of the game used for tournaments in France. It has been tried a few times in the UK but has never proved popular, and you will be most unlikely to come across it unless you cross the Channel (where they will sneakily place you at the additional disadvantage of having to play in French).

A few other unofficial variations of Scrabble have emerged. **If Only** allows you to turn one of your tiles over each shot and use it as a blank, as long as you score at least fifty. You can then replace that "blank" later with the letter it represents, and reuse the original tile. For instance, you play **SQUEEZE** with the **Z** represented by a tile turned over to look like a blank. You, but not your opponent, know that the tile is really a **K**. Later in the game, your rack reads **JHUCZLE**. You place the **Z**, right way up, in

SQUEEZE, lifting the **K**. Then you turn your **J** over to look like a blank, call it a **C**, and hey presto – the semantic mishmash of **JHUCZLE** becomes **CHUCKLE**.

If Only is a fast, open form of the game with bonuses aplenty and very high scores. It's useful for honing your bonus-finding skills, and as players generally enjoy this aspect of the game more than the board-blocking negative side, If Only friendlies are often played at tournaments at the end of the day as a wind-down from the rigours of the official games.

Some time ago, an Australian player came up with **Super Scrabble**. He cut a number of Scrabble boards into sections and created a larger board, something like 25x25 as against the standard 15x15. He added Quadruple and even Quintuple Letter and Word Squares, and played with two or perhaps three full sets of tiles. I believe there was even a 'wrap-around' option, where, if you came to the end of the row or bottom of the column, you could continue your word by going back to the beginning of the row or top of the column, if the space was free. Super Scrabble would take a long time to play and, with only a limited number of players prepared to mutilate their boards in its cause, it has remained more of a theoretical curiosity than a seriously-played game.

Finally, I can add my own modest creation to the panoply of Scrabble-related games with **Scrabble Poker**, a combination of Scrabble and my other favourite game, though one at which I remain distressingly and impoverishingly inept, poker. Each player picks, or is dealt, two tiles face down and one face up. There is then a round of betting in normal poker fashion, with each player calling, raising or folding as he or she sees fit. Another four tiles are dealt to each player, face up, with a further round of betting at the conclusion of each round of dealing.

When each player has seven tiles, five open and the other two known only to the holder, there is a final round of betting. The winner is the player who can make the longest word from his or her seven tiles (unlike real poker, you can use all seven to make your hand, not just your best five). In the event of two or more players making words of equal length, the winner is the one whose word has the highest face value.

It may never take the casinos or the on-line poker sites by storm, but I and a few of my friends like it as an occasional alternative to the Full Scrabble Monty, as it were. The civilizing influence of Scrabble tends to ensure stakes stay as pennies rather than pounds, and it's another good exercise in bonus-spotting, as well as giving practice in five- and six-letter words, which can sometimes get rather swept aside in the real game in the rush to master twos, threes, and fours, and to learn large numbers of ever more unlikely sevens.

None of these alternatives will ever usurp the genuine article from its position of supremacy, remaining rather the boisterous offspring of a serene and untroubled mother. Difficult enough to be challenging, yet not so arcane as to be open only to a select few, sociable, with the right combination of luck and skill, it can be tinkered with, but not improved upon. It is a tribute to the original game that it can admit so many other versions yet still remain effortlesly superior to all of them.

13 Help with Unusual Letter Combinations

A challenge that every Scrabble player faces at some point in almost every game is dealing with an unpromising combination of letters on their rack. Having too many of the same letter, too many vowels or too many consonants can put you in a situation where it is very difficult to come up with a viable word, let alone a high-scoring one.

This section contains various lists that may prove useful in dealing with an awkward combination of tiles, because they consist of words with unusual letter combinations.

Unusual Letter Combinations

Words from World English

One method of dealing with the awkward tile combinations that inevitably appear on your rack at some point in a game is to memorize a wide selection of words outside the core vocabulary of English. As the most widely spoken language in the world, English is rich in loan-words from other languages, and the versatility of the Roman alphabet and of English pronunciation means that these words tend to be assimilated without much corruption of their original sound. This means that there are many words in English that use 'foreign' letter combinations, which are ideal for Scrabble players. The following lists contain words from Australia, Canada, New Zealand and South Africa, as well as words from the main languages of the Indian Subcontinent – Hindi and Urdu – which have entered British English.

Australian words

Australian English is distinguished not only by the numerous Aboriginal terms for Australia's flora and fauna, but also by a great many shortened forms of commonplace English words. The Australian propensity to slang and short informal words is extremely useful to Scrabble players, especially as many of these words end in O, one of the most common tiles in the game. If you spot an O on the board when you have a difficult set of letters on your rack, there's a good chance that you'll be able to form an informal Aussie word. Native Australian words provide a range of unusual letter combinations, as well as a tendency to include double Os – ideal for rack balancing. Double Rs are also common in Australian English, as are Ks and Ys, so it's well worth acquiring some Antipodean vocabulary.

ADJIGO	yam plant		thing
ALF	an uncultivated Australian	**BELAH**	casuarina tree
ARVO	afternoon	**BERKO**	berserk
ASPRO	associate professor	**BIFFO**	fighting or aggressive
BARRO	embarrassing		behaviour
BAUERA	small evergreen shrub	**BILBY**	burrowing marsupial
BEAUT	outstanding person or	**BIZZO**	empty and irrelevant talk

BOAB	baobab tree		trousers
BODGIE	unruly or uncouth man	**DADAH**	illegal drugs
BOGAN	fool	**DAGGY**	untidy or dishevelled
BOOBOOK	small spotted brown owl	**DASYURE**	small carnivorous
BOOFY	strong but stupid		marsupial
BOONG	offensive word for a Black	**DELO**	delegate
	person	**DERRO**	vagrant
BOOSHIT	very good	**DINGO**	wild dog
BORA	native Australian coming-	**DINKUM**	genuine or right
	of-age ceremony	**DOCO**	documentary
BORAK	rubbish or nonsense	**DONGA**	steep-sided gully
BRASCO	lavatory	**DORBA**	stupid, inept, or clumsy
BROLGA	large grey crane with red-		person
	and-green head	**DRACK**	unattractive
BRUMBY	wild horse	**DRONGO**	slow-witted person
BUNYA	tall dome-shaped	**DROOB**	pathetic person
	coniferous tree	**DUBBO**	stupid
BUNYIP	legendary monster	**DUGITE**	venomous snake
CADAGI	tropical eucalyptus tree	**DURRY**	cigarette
CARBY	carburettor	**EARBASH**	talk incessantly
CHEWIE	chewing gum	**EMU**	large flightless bird
CHIACK	tease or banter	**EUMUNG**	type of acacia
CHOCO	conscript or militiaman	**EVO**	evening
CHOOK	hen or chicken	**EXO**	excellent
CHOOM	Englishman	**FASTIE**	deceitful act
COMMO	communist	**FESTY**	dirty or smelly
COMPO	compensation	**FIBRO**	house built of fibrocement
CORREA	evergreen shrub	**FIGJAM**	very conceited person
COUCAL	long-legged bird	**FIZGIG**	frivolous or flirtatious girl
COUGAN	rowdy person	**FOULIE**	bad mood
CRONK	unfit or unsound	**FRIB**	short heavy-conditioned
CROOL	spoil		piece of wool
CROWEA	pink-flowered shrub	**FUNDIE**	fundamentalist Christian
DACK	forcibly remove someone's	**FURPHY**	rumour or fictitious story

GALAH	grey-and-pink cockatoo	**LOPPY**	man employed to do
GARBO	dustman		maintenance work on a
GEEBUNG	tree with edible but		ranch
	tasteless fruit	**LOWAN**	ground-dwelling bird
GIDGEE	small acacia tree that	**LUBRA**	Aboriginal woman
	sometimes emits an	**MALLEE**	low shrubby eucalyptus
	unpleasant smell		tree
GILGAI	natural water hole	**MARRI**	type of eucalyptus
GING	child's catapult	**MIDDY**	middle-sized glass of beer
GNOW	ground-dwelling bird	**MILKO**	milkman
GOANNA	monitor lizard	**MOLOCH**	spiny lizard
GOOG	egg	**MOPOKE**	small spotted owl
GOOLIE	stone or pebble	**MOZ**	hoodoo or hex
GUNYAH	bush hut or shelter	**MUGGA**	eucalyptus tree with pink
GYMPIE	tall tree with stinging hairs		flowers and dark bark
	on its leaves	**MULGA**	acacia shrub
HAKEA	type of shrub or tree	**MULLOCK**	waste material from a
HOSTIE	air hostess		mine
HOVEA	plant with purple flowers	**MURREE**	native Australian
HUTCHIE	groundsheet draped over	**MURRI**	native Australian
	an upright stick as a	**MUSO**	musician
	temporary shelter	**MYALL**	native Australian living
JARRAH	type of eucalyptus tree		independently of society
JEFF	downsize or close down an	**MYXO**	myxomatosis
	organization	**NANA**	head
JUMBUCK	sheep	**NARDOO**	cloverlike fern
KARRI	type of eucalyptus tree	**NEDDY**	horse
KOALA	slow-moving arboreal	**NOAH**	shark
	marsupial	**NONG**	stupid or incompetent
KOORI	native Australian		person
KYBO	temporary lavatory	**NORK**	female breast
KYLIE	boomerang that is flat on	**NUDDY**	in the nude
	one side and convex on the	**NUMBAT**	small marsupial with long
	other		snout

OCKER	uncultivated or boorish Australian		group with short hair and distinctive clothes
PIKER	wild bullock	**SHERANG**	boss
PINDAN	desert region of Western Australia	**SHYPOO**	liquor of poor quality
		SITELLA	small black-and-white bird
PITURI	shrub with narcotic leaves	**SKEG**	rear fin on the underside of a surfboard
PLONKO	alcoholic, especially one who drinks wine	**SKITE**	boast
PLURRY	euphemism for bloody	**SMOKO**	cigarette break
PODDY	handfed calf or lamb	**SMOODGE**	smooch
POKIE	poker machine	**SPAG**	offensive term for an Italian
POON	stupid or ineffectual person	**SPRUIK**	speak in public
POONCE	male homosexual	**SWAGGIE**	vagrant worker
POSSIE	position	**SWAGMAN**	vagrant worker
PRELOVED	second-hand	**SWY**	a gambling game
QUOKKA	small wallaby	**TONK**	effeminate man
QUOLL	native cat	**TOOSHIE**	angry or upset
RAZOO	imaginary coin	**TRIELLA**	three horse races nominated for a bet
REFFO	offensive term for a European refugee after World War Two	**TROPPO**	mentally affected by a tropical climate
REGO	registration of a motor vehicle	**TRUCKIE**	truck driver
		TRUGO	game similar to croquet
RESTO	restored antique, vintage car, etc	**TUAN**	flying phalanger
		TUART	type of eucalyptus tree
ROO	kangaroo	**UMPIE**	umpire
ROUGHIE	something unfair, especially a trick	**UNCO**	awkward or clumsy
		UPTA	of poor quality
SANGER	sandwich	**UPTER**	of poor quality
SANGO	sandwich	**UTE**	utility
SCOZZA	rowdy person	**VAG**	vagrant
SCUNGY	miserable, sordid or dirty	**VEGO**	vegetarian
SHARPIE	a member of a teenage	**VIGORO**	women's game similar to

	cricket		blue spots
WADDY	heavy wooden club used by	**WOF**	fool or idiot
	native Australians	**WOMBAT**	burrowing marsupial
WAGGA	blanket made of sacks	**WOOMERA**	spear-throwing stick
	stitched together	**WURLEY**	Aboriginal hut
WALLABY	marsupial resembling a	**YABBER**	talk or jabber
	small kangaroo	**YABBY**	small freshwater crayfish
WANDOO	eucalyptus tree with white	**YACCA**	grass tree
	bark	**YACKA**	grass tree
WARATAH	shrub with dark green	**YARRAN**	small hardy tree
	leaves and crimson flowers	**YATE**	small eucalyptus tree
WARB	dirty or insignificant person	**YIKE**	argument, squabble or fight
WHARFIE	wharf labourer	**YUCKO**	disgusting
WIDGIE	female bodgie	**YUMMO**	delicious
WILGA	small drought-resistant tree	**ZAMBUCK**	St John ambulance
WIRILDA	acacia tree with edible		attendant
	seeds	**ZIFF**	beard
WIRRAH	saltwater fish with bright		

Canadian words

Canadian English combines a broad range of British and US terms with words derived from Inuit, as well as from other Native American languages such as Algonquin. Canadian English incorporates many Canadian French words from Quebec, and there are also a number of recently coined Canadian terms. Inuit words can be helpful to Scrabble players because they tend to be quite vowel-heavy. K occurs frequently in Inuit terms, and sometimes appears twice. Such words require a blank tile for the second K if they are to be played during a game.

AGLOO	breathing hole made in ice	**AMOWT**	hood on an Inuit woman's
	by a seal		parka for carrying a child
AGLU	breathing hole made in ice	**ATIGI**	Inuit parka
	by a seal	**BABICHE**	thongs or lacings of
AMAUT	hood on an Inuit woman's		rawhide
	parka for carrying a child	**BARACHOIS**	shallow lagoon formed by a

	sand bar	**KLOOTCH**	North American Indian
BATEAU	light flat-bottomed boat		woman
BEIGNET	deep-fried pastry	**KUDLIK**	Inuit soapstone seal-oil
BOGAN	sluggish side stream		lamp
BREWIS	Newfoundland cod stew	**LOGAN**	backwater
BUTTE	isolated steep-sided flat-	**LOONIE**	Canadian dollar coin with
	topped hill		loon bird on one face
CABOOSE	mobile bunkhouse used by	**MUCKAMUCK**	food
	lumbermen	**MUKTUK**	beluga skin used as food
CANOLA	cooking oil extracted from	**NANOOK**	polar bear
	a variety of rapeseed	**PARFLECHE**	dried rawhide
	developed in Canada	**PARKADE**	building used as a car park
CAYUSE	small Native American	**PARKETTE**	small public park
	pony used by cowboys	**PLEW**	beaver skin used as
COULEE	dry stream valley		standard unit in fur trading
CUSK	gadoid food fish	**POGEY**	financial relief for the
DEKE	act or instance of feinting		unemployed
	in ice hockey	**POGY**	financial relief for the
GROWLER	small iceberg that has		unemployed
	broken off from a larger	**POKELOGAN**	backwater
	iceberg or glacier	**POUTINE**	chipped potatoes topped
HONKER	Canada goose		with curd cheese and
HOSER	unsophisticated rural		tomato sauce
	person	**PUNG**	horse-drawn sleigh
ICEWINE	dessert wine made from	**REDEYE**	drink incorporating beer
	frozen grapes		and tomato juice
JIGGER	device used when setting a	**RUBABOO**	soup made by boiling
	gill net beneath ice		pemmican
JOUAL	nonstandard Canadian	**RUBBY**	rubbing alcohol mixed with
	French dialect		cheap wine for drinking
KAMIK	Inuit boot made of caribou	**SKOOKUM**	strong or brave
	hide or sealskin	**SNYE**	side channel of a river
KLOOCH	North American Indian	**SPLAKE**	hybrid trout bred by
	woman		Canadian zoologists

SWILER	seal hunter	**TUPEK**	Inuit tent of animal skins
TILLICUM	friend	**TUPIK**	Inuit tent of animal skins
TOONIE	Canadian two-dollar coin	**TWONIE**	Canadian two-dollar coin
TULLIBEE	whitefish found in the Great Lakes	**WAWA**	speech or language
		WENDIGO	evil spirit or cannibal

Hindi words

After Chinese, Hindi, the dominant language of India, is the most widely spoken language in the world. Many Hindi words entered British English during the Raj, and some have become everyday terms – bungalow and pundit, for example. Others are less common, but are useful to Scrabble players because they provide unusual letter combinations and thus solutions to difficult racks. Combinations such as BH, DH and KH are common in Hindi-derived words, and the preponderance of As, Is and Us can be very helpful in trying to balance a vowel-heavy rack. Above all, Hindi words are useful because they are quite unusual, and so provide a range of options for Scrabble players that aren't immediately obvious – front-hooking onto hang with a B, for example, or end-hookin onto punk with an A. Committing some Hindi-derived words to memory will help to keep your opponents on their toes.

AKHARA	gymnasium	**BHANG**	psychoactive drug made of hemp
ALAP	vocal music without words		
AMBARY	tropical plant	**BHANGRA**	music combining traditional Punjabi music with Western pop
ANKUS	elephant goad		
ANNA	old copper coin		
ARTI	Hindu ritual	**BHAVAN**	large house or building
AYAH	maidservant or nursemaid	**BHEESTY**	water-carrier
BABU	Mr	**BHINDI**	okra used in cooking
BAEL	spiny tree	**BHISHTI**	water-carrier
BAHADUR	title for distinguished Indians during the Raj	**BINDI**	decorative dot in middle of forehead
BANDH	general strike	**BOBBERY**	mixed pack of hunting dogs
BANYAN	tree with aerial roots		
BHAJI	deep-fried vegetable savoury	**BUND**	embankment
		CHAI	tea, especially with added

	spices	**CRORE**	ten million
CHAMPAC	tree with fragrant yellow	**CUSHY**	comfortable
	flowers	**DACOIT**	a member of a gang of
CHAPATI	flat coarse unleavened		armed robbers
	bread	**DACOITY**	robbery by an armed gang
CHAPPAL	sandal	**DAK**	system of mail delivery
CHARAS	hashish	**DAL**	split grain
CHARKHA	spinning wheel	**DATURA**	plant with trumpet-shaped
CHEETAH	large swift feline mammal		flowers
CHETAH	large swift feline mammal	**DEKKO**	look or glance
CHELA	disciple of a religious	**DEODAR**	Himalayan cedar
	teacher	**DEWAN**	chief minister of an Indian
CHICHI	person of mixed British and		princedom
	Indian descent	**DHAK**	tropical tree with red
CHILLUM	pipe for smoking cannabis		flowers
CHINTZ	printed cotton with glazed	**DHAL**	curry made from lentils
	finish	**DHARNA**	method of obtaining
CHITAL	the axis deer		justice by fasting
CHOKEY	prison	**DHOBI**	washerman
CHOLI	short-sleeved bodice	**DHOTI**	loincloth
CHOWK	marketplace	**DUPATTA**	scarf
CHUDDAR	large shawl or veil	**DURBAR**	court of an Indian ruler
CHUDDIES	underpants	**DURRIE**	cotton carpet
CHUKAR	Indian partridge	**DURZI**	Indian tailor
CHUKKA	period of play in polo	**GANJA**	potent form of cannabis
CHUTNEY	Indian pickle	**GAUR**	large wild cow
COOLIE	cheaply hired unskilled	**GARIAL**	fish-eating crocodilian with
	labourer		long slender snout
COOLY	cheaply hired unskilled	**GAVIAL**	fish-eating crocodilian with
	labourer		long slender snout
COWAGE	tropical climbing plant with	**GHARIAL**	fish-eating crocodilian with
	stinging pods		long slender snout
COWHAGE	tropical climbing plant with	**GHARRI**	horse-drawn vehicle for
	stinging pods		hire

GHARRY	horse-drawn vehicle for hire	**KULFI**	Indian dessert
GHAT	stairs or passage leading down to a river	**KURTA**	long loose garment like a shirt without a collar
GHEE	clarified butter	**LAC**	resinous substance secreted by insects
GHERAO	industrial action in which workers imprison their employers	**LAKH**	100,000
		LANGUR	arboreal monkey
		LASSI	yoghurt drink
GINGILI	oil obtained from sesame seeds	**LATHI**	long heavy stick used as a weapon
GORAL	small goat antelope	**LUNGI**	long piece of cloth worn as loincloth or turban
GUAR	plant that produces gum		
GUNNY	coarse fabric used for sacks	**MACHAN**	platform used in tiger hunting
GURU	Hindu or Sikh religious teacher	**MAHOUT**	elephant driver
HARTAL	act of closing shop or stopping work as a political protest	**MAHSEER**	large freshwater fish
		MANDI	big market
		MANDIR	Hindu or Jain temple
HOWDAH	seat for riding on an elephant's back	**MAUND**	unit of weight
		MEHNDI	practice of painting designs on the hands and feet using henna
JAGGERY	coarse brown sugar		
JAI	victory		
KHADDAR	cotton cloth	**MELA**	cultural or religious festival
KHEDA	enclosure for captured elephants	**MOHUR**	old gold coin
		MONAL	Asian pheasant
KHEDAH	enclosure for captured elephants	**MORCHA**	hostile demonstration against the government
KHEDDAH	enclosure for captured elephants	**MRIDANG**	drum used in Indian music
		MYNAH	tropical starling
KOEL	parasitic cuckoo	**NAUCH**	intricate Indian dance
KOS	Indian unit of distance	**NAUTCH**	intricate Indian dance
KRAIT	brightly coloured venomous snake	**NAWAB**	Muslim prince in India
		NEEM	large tree
KUKRI	Ghurka knife	**NILGAI**	large Indian antelope

NULLAH	stream or drain	**RUPEE**	standard monetary unit of India
NUMDAH	coarse felt		
OONT	camel	**RUPIAH**	standard monetary unit of Indonesia
PACHISI	game resembling backgammon		
		RYOT	peasant or tenant farmer
PAISA	one hundredth of a rupee	**SAMBAR**	deer with three-tined antlers
PAKORA	dish of deep-fried chicken or vegetables		
		SAMITI	political association
PANEER	soft white cheese	**SAMOSA**	triangular pastry containing spiced vegetables or meat
PARATHA	flat unleavened bread		
PEEPUL	tree similar to the banyan		
PUNKA	fan made of palm leaves	**SARANGI**	stringed instrument played with a bow
PUNKAH	fan made of palm leaves		
PURDA	custom of keeping women secluded	**SARDAR**	Sikh title
		SARI	traditional dress of Indian women
PURDAH	custom of keeping women secluded		
		SAROD	Indian stringed instrument
PURI	unleavened flaky bread	**SWAMI**	title for a Hindu saint or religious teacher
PUTTEE	strip of cloth wound around the leg		
		TABLA	pair of drums whose pitches can be varied
RAGGEE	cereal grass		
RAGI	cereal grass	**THALI**	meal consisting of several small dishes
RAITA	yoghurt-and-vegetable dish served with curry		
		TIL	sesame
RAJ	government	**TOLA**	unit of weight
RAJAH	ruler or landlord	**TONGA**	light two-wheeled vehicle
RAMTIL	African plant grown in India	**TOPEE**	pith helmet
		TOPI	pith helmet
RANEE	queen or princess	**URD**	bean plant
RANI	queen or princess	**VAHANA**	vehicle in Indian myth
RATHA	four-wheeled carriage drawn by horses or bullocks	**VANDA**	type of orchid
		VINA	stringed musical instrument
ROTI	type of unleavened bread	**WALLAH**	person in charge of a

ZENANA	specific thing part of a house reserved for women and girls	**ZILLA**	administrative district in India
ZILA	administrative district in India	**ZILLAH**	administrative district in India

New Zealand

While New Zealand and Australian English have many words in common, the Kiwi lexicon is greatly enriched by New Zealand's Maori heritage. Maori-derived words are a marvellous resource for the Scrabble player, providing a wealth of unusual vowel combinations, and frequently using consonants that are rarer in European words, such as K, W and H. Maori words are especially good for balancing vowel-heavy racks, as many words use several As, Us or Is – sometimes with three vowels in a row. Relatively high-scoring consonants are also very common, especially K and H. Unfortunately, there is only one K in Scrabble, so many Maori words with two Ks are less useful than they might initially appear. Don't forget blank tiles, however: if you have a blank, a K and a couple of vowels on your rack, there's a good chance that you can find a New Zealand word to play profitably. There are also some unusual words that have entered the vocabulary of New Zealanders from European or Asian languages.

ATUA	spirit or demon	**HUHU**	hairy beetle
BOOHAI	thoroughly lost	**HUI**	conference or meeting
COOTIE	body louse	**HUIA**	extinct New Zealand bird
GOORIE	mongrel dog	**JAFA**	offensive term for
GRAUNCH	crush or destroy		someone from Auckland
HAKA	war dance	**JANOLA**	household bleach
HANGI	open-air cooking pit	**KAHAWAI**	large fish
HAPU	subtribe	**KAI**	food
HAPUKA	large fish	**KAIK**	village
HAPUKU	large fish	**KAINGA**	village
HEITIKI	neck ornament	**KAKA**	long-billed parrot
HIKOI	protest march	**KAKAPO**	ground-dwelling parrot
HOKONUI	illicit whisky	**KARAKIA**	prayer
HONGI	nose-touching greeting	**KARANGA**	call or chant of welcome

KATIPO	small venomous spider		compensation
KAUPAPA	strategy, policy or cause	**PIKAU**	rucksack
KAURI	coniferous tree	**PIPI**	shellfish
KAWA	protocol or etiquette	**PIUPIU**	leaf skirt
KIEKIE	climbing bush plant	**POI**	ball of woven flax
KIWI	flightless bird with long beak and no tail	**PONGA**	tall tree fern
		PORAE	edible sea fish
KOHA	gift or donation	**PORANGI**	crazy
KOKAKO	long-tailed crow	**PORINA**	moth larva
KONEKE	farm vehicle	**POTAE**	hat
KORU	curved pattern	**POWHIRI**	welcoming ceremony
KOWHAI	small tree	**PUGGY**	sticky
KUIA	female elder	**PUHA**	sow thistle
KURI	mongrel dog	**PUKEKO**	wading bird
KUTU	body louse	**PURIRI**	forest tree
MANUKA	myrtaceous tree	**RAHUI**	Maori prohibition
MATAI	evergreen tree	**RATA**	myrtaceous forest tree
MIHI	ceremonial greeting	**RAUPATU**	seizure of land
MOA	extinct large flightless bird	**RAURIKI**	sow thistle
MOKI	edible sea fish	**SHEEPO**	person who brings sheep to the catching pen for shearing
MOKO	Maori tattoo or tattoo pattern		
MOOLOO	person from Waikato	**TAIAHA**	ceremonial fighting staff
MOPOKE	small spotted owl	**TAIHOA**	hold on!
MUNGA	army canteen	**TAKAHE**	rare flightless bird
NGAIO	small tree	**TANGI**	Maori funeral ceremony
NGATI	tribe or clan	**TANIWHA**	legendary monster
NIKAU	palm tree	**TAONGA**	treasure
PAKAHI	acid soil or land	**TAPU**	sacred or forbidden
PAKAPOO	Chinese lottery	**TARSEAL**	bitumen surface of a road
PAKOKO	small freshwater fish	**TAUIWI**	non-Maori people of New Zealand
PAUA	edible abalone		
PERFING	early retirement from the police force with financial	**TIKANGA**	Maori customs
		TOETOE	type of tall grass

TOITOI	type of tall grass	**WETA**	long-legged wingless
TWINK	white correction fluid		insect
WAKA	Maori canoe	**WHANAU**	family
WEKA	flightless bird	**WHENAU**	native land
WERO	warrior's challenge		

South Africa

South African English includes words from Nguni languages such as Xhosa and Zulu, as well as Afrikaans, amongst other languages. For Scrabble players, South African English offers a host of useful words for balancing vowel-heavy racks. Many Afrikaans-derived words contain a double A, while Nguni words often contain two or three As. It's a good idea, therefore, to have some South African words up your sleeve for when you find yourself with two or more As on your rack. There are also a lot of K words in South African English. As K can be an awkward letter to use effectively, these can come in very handy, as can the Afrikaans-derived words containing V, which are most helpful in trying to use a difficult tile.

AMADODA	grown men	**JONG**	friend
AMANDLA	politcal slogan calling for	**KAAL**	naked
	power to the Black	**KEREL**	chap or fellow
	population	**KRAAL**	stockaded village
BAAS	boss	**KWAITO**	type of pop music
BABALAS	drunk or hungover	**LEGUAAN**	large monitor lizard
BAKKIE	small truck	**MEERKAT**	sociable mongoose
BRAAI	grill or roast meat	**MENEER**	Mr or sir
BRAAIVLEIS	barbecue	**MEVROU**	Mrs or madam
BUNDU	wild, remote region	**MOOI**	pleasing
DAGGA	marijuana	**MUTI**	herbal medicine
DWAAL	state of befuddlement	**NAARTJIE**	tangerine
GEELBEK	yellow-jawed fish	**NEK**	mountain pass
HAMBA	go away	**NKOSI**	master or chief
JA	yes	**OKE**	man
JAAP	simpleton	**OOM**	title of respect
JEREPIGO	heavy desert wine	**OUBAAS**	person senior in rank or

		STEEN	variety of white grape
	years	STOKVEL	savings pool or syndicate
PADKOS	snacks for a long journey	VLEI	area of marshy ground
PLAAS	farm	VOEMA	vigour or energy
ROOIKAT	lynx	VOETSEK	expression of dismissal or rejection
SCAMTO	argot of urban South African Blacks		
SKOLLY	hooligan	VROU	woman or wife
SNOEK	edible marine fish	YEBO	yes
SPEK	bacon, fat or fatty pork		

Urdu words

Urdu, the official language of Pakistan and one of the official languages of India, is closely related to Hindi. Urdu, however, contains many more words derived from Arabic and Persian, and also uses a different system of writing from Hindi, lending a different character to the words that have entered English. Many Urdu culinary terms will be familiar to British Scrabble players from Indian restaurants, while most Anglo-Indian military vocabulary also derives from Urdu rather than Hindi. As with Hindi, the variant spellings of many Urdu words provide opportunities for Scrabble players, as does the frequency of the letter K.

BAGH	garden	CHARPAI	bedstead of woven webbing on a wooden frame
BALTI	spicy Indian dish stewed until most liquid has evaporated	CHARPOY	bedstead of woven webbing on a wooden frame
BASTI	slum	DAROGHA	manager
BEGUM	woman of high rank	DHANSAK	Indian dish of meat or vegetables braised with lentils
BIRIANI	Indian dish of highly flavoured rice mixed with meat or fish		
BIRYANI	Indian dish of highly flavoured rice mixed with meat or fish	INQILAB	revolution
		IZZAT	honour or prestige
BUSTEE	slum	JACONET	light cotton fabric
BUSTI	slum	JEMADAR	officer in the Indian police

KAMEEZ	long tunic		yoghurt or cream
KEBAB	dish of meat, onions, etc, grilled on skewers	**RABI**	crop harvested at the end of winter
KHAKI	dull yellowish-brown colour	**SAHIB**	title placed after a man's name
KHARIF	crop harvested at beginning of winter	**SAICE**	servant who looks after horses
KHAYAL	kind of Indian classical vocal music	**SARPANCH**	head of a village council
		SEPOY	Indian soldier in the service of the British
KINCOB	fine silk fabric embroidered with gold or silver threads	**SHALWAR**	loose-fitting trousers
KOFTA	Indian dish of seasoned minced meat shaped into balls	**SHIKAR**	hunting
		SHIKAREE	hunter
		SHIKARI	hunter
KOFTGAR	person skilled in inlaying steel with gold	**SICE**	servant who looks after horses
KOFTGARI	art of inlaying steel with gold	**SUBADAH**	chief native office in a company of sepoys
KORMA	Indian dish of meat or vegetables braised with yoghurt or cream	**SUBADAR**	chief native office in a company of sepoys
		SUBAH	chief native office in a company of sepoys
LASCAR	sailor from the East Indies		
MAIDAN	open space used for meetings and sports	**SYCE**	servant who looks after horses
MASALA	mixed spices ground into a paste	**TAHSIL**	administrative division
		TALOOKA	subdivision of a district
MOOLVI	Muslim doctor of the law	**TALUK**	subdivision of a district
MOOLVIE	Muslim doctor of the law	**TALUKA**	subdivision of a district
MURDABAD	down with; death to	**TAMASHA**	show or entertainment
MUSTH	frenzied sexual excitement in male elephants	**TANDOORI**	method of cooking on a spit in a clay oven
NUMDAH	coarse felt		
QORMA	Indian dish of meat or vegetables braised with		

Glossary of terms

Only terms used in this book are included.

ABSP The Association of British Scrabble Players, the official organization which regulates tournament play and carries out other associated functions.

Affix A prefix or suffix.

Anagram A word which comprises the same letters as another word, but in a different order.

Big tiles The high-scoring tiles – **J**, **Q**, **X**, and **Z**. In some contexts also includes the **S**'s and blanks.

Blank One of two tiles in the set which the holder may use to represent any letter.

Block To play a move which prevents an opponent from playing in that part of the board.

Blocked board or **game** A board with few positions where moves are possible. Opposite of **open board** or **game**.

Blocker A move which prevents an opponent from playing, either a specific move or in a particular part of the board; a word which cannot be extended either at the front or the back.

Bonus The extra fifty points awarded for playing all seven tiles in one move; a move which achieves this.

Break up To play some of a promising combination of letters.

Challenge To query the validity of a word played by an opponent. The word must then be checked in a dictionary or Scrabble word book.

Change To use one's turn by putting unwanted tiles back into the bag and picking new ones, rather than by placing a move on the board.

Combination Any stated group of letters.

Common letter A low-scoring letter of which there are several in the set; a letter which is part of a word on the board both horizontally and vertically.

Compound word A word made out of two smaller words, which combines the meanings of both of them.

Consonant-heavy Describes a rack with too many consonants.

Contraction A word formed from a longer word, but with some of the letters omitted, although the meaning is unchanged.

Glossary of terms

*Count noun A noun representing something of which there can be one or more than one, e.g. table. Opposite of mass noun.

Criss-Crosswords The name of an early version of Scrabble.

Crosswise play The playing of a move which creates only one new word on the board. Opposite of **parallel play**.

Discard (tiles) To replace unwanted tiles in the bag, in order to draw new ones. Now done only when changing, but a regular move in earlier versions of the game.

Distribution The frequency with which each letter appears in a standard set of tiles.

Double letter (score) A square, on most boards coloured light blue, which doubles the point value of any tile played on it.

Double word (score) A square, on most boards coloured pink, which doubles the point value of any word which has one of its letters on it.

Draw (tiles) To pick tiles from the bag.

Duplicate The same letter appearing two or more times on the same rack.

Endgame The final stages of a game, when knowledge of the letters which are or may be on an opponent's rack affects the moves a player makes.

End hook A letter which can be placed at the end of a word to make another word.

Face value The number of points scored by any tile, word, or move, unaffected by Premium Squares.

Floater A tile on the board, in such a position that it can be used as part of another word.

Frequency The number of times a given letter appears in a standard set.

Front hook A letter which can be placed at the beginning of a word to make another word.

Hook A letter which can be placed at the beginning or end of a word to make another word; to play a move which uses a letter in this way.

Interlocking Joining tiles to those already on the board to make new words; all moves in a game except the opening move must be interlocking.

It The name of an early version of Scrabble.

Leave (the) The tiles left on a player's rack, after playing a move but before picking fresh tiles from the bag.

Lexiko The name of the original version of Scrabble.

*Mass noun A noun representing something which cannot be counted, e.g. fairness. Opposite of count noun.

Matchplay Playing solely to win the game, without relevance to the score achieved.

Nine-timer A word which covers two Triple Word squares, and therefore has its point value multiplied by nine.

One-pointer A tile worth one point, i.e. the commonest letters most useful for making bonus words – **AEILNORSTU**.

Open board or **game** A board with several positions where moves, especially high-scoring moves, are possible. Opposite of **blocked board** or **game**.

OSW (Official Scrabble Words) A book containing an alphabetical listing of all allowable words for Scrabble.

Outplay A move which enables a player to play all his or her remaining tiles, there being no more tiles left in the bag – therefore, the last move of the game.

Parallel play A move in which a word is placed parallel to another word or words on the board, thus also forming one or more vertical words if the main word is played horizontally, and vice versa. Opposite of **crosswise play**.

Play out To play all one's remaining tiles, there being no more tiles left in the bag, thus playing the last move of the game.

Point value The number of points scored by a given tile.

Prefix A combination of letters which can often be found at the beginning of a word.

Premium square A square on the board which awards more than face value to a letter or word played on it – a Double Letter, Double Word, Triple Letter, or Triple Word score.

Rack The wooden or plastic stand on which a player places his or her tiles; the letters held by a player at any particular time.

Rack management The playing of tiles in such a way as to increase one's chances of having a bonus word, or other high-scoring move, on the next or subsequent turn.

Ratings A system for ranking players who take part in ABSP tournaments, so that the best players can be established and all players can assess their relative progress.

Runner An assistant at a tournament, whose job is to take challenge sheets to the Tournament Director or other appointed person for adjudication, then return the sheet to the players concerned.

'Six plus one' list A list of seven-letter words which can be formed by the addition of one other letter to a particular combination of six letters. Similarly **'six plus two' list** or **'seven plus one' list**.

Spread In a game or tournament, the total number of points scored by a player, minus the total points scored against him or her. A spread may therefore be positive or negative.

Suffix A combination of letters which can often be found at the end of a word.

Sum of Opponents' Scores The total number of wins achieved by all of a player's opponents in a tournament – formerly used to separate players on the same number of wins, but now replaced by spread.

Swiss system A method of organizing fixtures at large tournaments, where each player is, as far as possible, matched against another on the same number of wins.

Synergy The property of certain combinations of letters of combining well with each other to form words.

Take A word is said to take a particular letter when that letter can be added to the word to form another word. A word may take a letter at the front or at the end.

Tile Any of the one hundred pieces, each (except the two blanks) representing a letter, which are used to play the game by forming words on the board.

Tile-tracking Noting which tiles have been played, and modifying one's play accordingly to take account of which tiles are likely to be picked or which tiles the opponent is, or may be, holding.

Tournament Director The person responsible for ensuring a tournament is run according to the rules, and who arbitrates in any disputes between players.

Triple letter (score) A square, on most boards coloured dark blue, which triples the point value of any letter played on it.

Triple word (score) A square, on most boards coloured red, which triples the point value of any word which has one of its letters on it.

Vowel-consonant balance or **vowel-consonant split** The number of vowels and consonants on the rack, or remaining in the bag, at any particular time.

Vowel-heavy Describes a rack with too many vowels.

Z-three A three-letter word containing a **Z**.

Answers to puzzles

CHALLENGE NO. 1

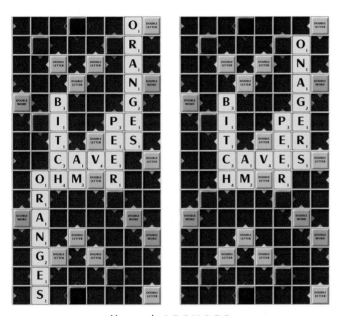

Your rack: **A E G N O R S**

Finding **ORANGES** should not have presented you with too much of a problem. But the importance of the two- and three-letter words is shown by the fact that you can't fit **ORANGES** in without either remembering **PE** and **ES**, or noticing that unlikely hook of turning **HM** into **OHM**.

Incidentally, both those moves put a letter in an outer row of the board, and thus open up a possible nine-timer – a word stretching from one Triple Word Square to the next, thus having its score multiplied by nine as well as scoring the extra fifty, probably scoring about 150 for one move. This is undesirable, because your opponent gets first crack at it, and if your opponent has also been nursing his or her rack towards a bonus, they might just be ready to step in. That shouldn't stop you from playing **ORANGES** if it's the only bonus you can see, but you'd be better, if you know it, to play **ONAGERS**, in the same column as **ORANGES/PE/ES** but one square down, also making **PE**, **ER** and **CAVES**. That not only scores more but also, and more importantly, doesn't open the nine-timer.

An onager is a type of wild ass, but what you should try to remember is the fact that it's an anagram of **ORANGES**, so that next time you find **ORANGES** on your rack, you will have a bigger choice of moves to play.

CHALLENGE NO. 2

Your rack: **D E I J N O S**

Notice how the short word comfortably outscores the longer one, and, in this case, also prevens your opponent from getting much profit out of the Triple Word squares in the top row.

CHALLENGE NO. 3

Your rack: **A E L M Q S U**

Playing **QUALM** opens a bonus spot along the bottom row, and it may be better to forego ten points by restricting your play to **QUA**. If your opponent's last move was just playing an **N** after **PI** to make **PIN** for six points, it looks like he or she is close to a bonus so **QUA** might be more sensible. Indeed, taking out one of the high-scoring bonus spots by playing **QUALMS** or **SQUEAL** might be more sensible still. If, on the other hand, your opponent has just played **ZO/HO** for 27, he or she probably played for the points and is less likely to have a bonus rack now. Your move will depend on how defensive you want to be, how good you think your opponent is, and what sort of a feeling you've got in your water about the whole position.

CHALLENGE NO. 4

Your rack: **B D O R R S ?**

The blank is pretty clearly going to have to be a vowel, and **E** is the most likely, especially with the duplicate R. Note that, even if your opponent played **QUINE** and you didn't know it, you do know **EQUINE**, and you're every bit as entitled to play it as old smarty-pants on the other side of the table.